Getting The Most Out of Teams

By

J. Kenneth Boggs

ISBN: 1-4033-2919-2 (E-book)
ISBN: 1-4033-2920-6 (Paperback)
ISBN: 1-4033-2921-4 (Hardcover)

Library of Congress Control Number: 2002105681

This book is printed on acid free paper.

Printed in the United States of America
Bloomington, IN

1stBooks - rev. 10/29/02

Table of Contents

Preface

As Al Pacino said in the first *Godfather* movie, "...let me make you an offer you can't refuse..." for within this book you will find team member skills and leadership skills distilled to their essence. Though there is a great deal that can be said on these two topics, the essential basics are no longer a mystery and are now out in the open for all to see and take advantage of.

I became captive of this material early in my nearly thirty-eight year career in IBM where I worked in marketing, software and hardware product development, brand management, and services. I was concerned with what I saw inside IBM where the best and the brightest consistently failed to live up to their potential - and worked long hours to do so.

I also became concerned by newspaper reports of conditions outside IBM that sounded familiar.

- During a period of major growth in productivity, organizations struggling to get or remain profitable.

- Middle managers finding themselves with too much to do, to many demands, and unable to do all that they know is important.

- Lower level, non-management employees fearing there is no career path, no pension, no continuing health care, and no way out.

  It sounded like increasingly like the business world was approaching a sweatshop mentality.

- Polarization of superficially different views on almost every subject in our society.

I had a deep belief that all the resources were already present - human and other - to do much better than was evident on the evening TV news. There had to be a way for people to work better together and to be more effectively led.

I was most fortunate to be in a position to observe, experiment, brainstorm and discuss ideas with kindred souls, and eventually discover what was in front of us all the time like a purloined letter. My intuitive sense gave me the patience, interest and energy to discover the obvious - no one had crawled inside teams and asked what was needed from the viewpoint of the people involved.

Once I had sorted out the team processes I was delighted to read **Built To Last - Successful Habits of Visionary Companies** by James C. Collins and Jerry I. Porras who had done extensive research on what leadership produces visible outstanding corporate results. Their insights and observations helped me to complete my own work on leadership begun in my study of teams.

Last I put these two pieces together as they should have been from the start since they are quite interwoven in may ways. All that it took from there was to spend several years writing, receiving critical feedback and rewriting. It has been a struggle to get my thoughts down clearly. I hope I have done so and if not invite interaction, discussion and feedback to improve the clarity.

The value of this book is that it has packaged all this insight and learning into a very small bundle. Now the magic is available to everyone. So read on and good luck. Be patient with your understanding, apply what you understand right now and take time out regularly to assess what you have learned. Continual progress is not assured to those who are passive but it is guaranteed to those who follow the process laid out.

Acknowledgments

Since I began writing this material back in 1992, many people - an extended team—has helped me in a variety of ways. I want to explicitly thank as many as I can recall and apologize to those I have forgotten.

- Mary Lucas is my "creek buddy", friend, confidant and wife without whose support, patience and encouragement I could never have finished this project.

- Thanks to Holly, Stacie, Shelley and Heather - my four daughters - who gave me the opportunity to experiment with a "live in" team. Special thanks to Stacie and Shelley for being proofreaders and editors.

- Thanks goes to my brother-in-law, Dick Gazley, for giving one of my drafts a thorough editing. Thanks to his wife, my sister, for supporting this process.

- Great appreciation goes to the IBM Corporation that has meant more than just income and career for me. IBM has also been family, laboratory and friend.

- Thanks to Arthur Moore, an IBM associate, who operated as my sounding board and provided me challenging arguments. Arthur helped me to do the difficult task of distilling down the variety of behaviors expressed by both teams and leaders.

- Thanks to Douglas Storey of the Catalog Literary Agency in Vancouver, WA as he saw promise in my initial book on these subjects.

- Thanks to the Project Management Institute who gave me critical feedback on my initial book and as a result of which I have been able to improve clarity, readability and ease of use.

- Thanks to the people who have allowed me to be their mentor and leader. Their trust has allowed me to grow and learn while their accomplishments have given me great joy and satisfaction.

- Thanks to the many teams that have included me and given me a chance to perform and to learn about teams.

Having given my special thanks, I want to make it clear that any "misteaks" are mine and mine alone. I hope I have done justice to my subject and my readers.

Introduction

This book debunks and challenges many commonly held views and popular myths about leadership and teams. So when swimming against the current viewpoint it seems appropriate to take a moment and establish who this book is directed towards, to define what is meant by a team and what teams are thus covered, to define what is meant by leadership and what leadership is covered, and to hear from a few who have already used this material to get a glimpse of that experience.

Audience

Who can make use of and benefit from the material covered in this book? Virtually everyone I think. For starters anyone who is either an employee or employer. Additionally folks who find themselves organizing groups of people, including children.

Most important the people who can make use of this material are, pardon my expression, ordinary. It does not take someone with a college degree or someone as trained as an Olympic athlete. All of us are candidates to benefit both as team members as well in our roles as leaders.

Some might think they only work by themselves and therefore never have the opportunity to work on a team. But unless you are a hermit hiding in the back woods, all of us interact with many people who provide us service. In these interactions we can choose to operate as cooperative peers who both have something to give and to gain, i.e. a small team. Too in these interactions we are the initiators who know what they want from the interaction, i.e. a leader.

Teams

It is commonplace to find ourselves operating in various teams. Work asks for us to "get on board and be a team member". At church we find ourselves on a ruling board. In our volunteer activities we are assigned to a committee. In many situations we are challenged be an effective individual but do that while interacting with others in this grouping called a team. But experience with these teams varies.

Some experience with teams has been unsatisfactory. Some people avoid teams and see them as time consuming, dragging down good people's performance. One classic business negative stereotype is the business meeting that goes on at length and results in no obvious useful output. The Dilbert comic strip entertains many with these kinds of examples. It is obvious that creating useful and efficient teams is not all that easy. Many might seek the help of what has been already written.

Much work has been published on the subject of teams, team development, managing teams and team leadership. It would appear that this is a tired subject. Unfortunately everything so far has approached teams from outside the team, from a manager's viewpoint and not that of the team member. The approach so far seems to make the assumption that someone outside the team can maximize the team and make the team do what it was assembled for. This viewpoint might be valid where the people managed are not the intellectual and emotional peers of the manager but that is generally not the case in the American society. Thus a different mindset needs to be taken.

Our approach here is to get inside the team and explore what a team member does that is most helpful and which contributes to optimal team performance. Clearly it is the team members' behavior and how it interacts with other team members that constitutes the results of the team. Thus, we focus on the individual team member's contribution exploring what is needed to optimize various behaviors and interactions with the expectation that results too will be maximized. However this too is not sufficient since teams do not operate in a vacuum.

Influences from outside the team are important and are separately investigated. This material can give managers and leaders guidance about how their behavior can maximize the results of the team.

The reason that all this material has been collected is that in combination--a high performing team with a highly effective manager--the organizational results far exceed any other approach described heretofore. The combination also maximizes satisfaction of the team members and maximizes the results of the team while establishing realistic confidence so that the results are repeatable and sustainable. This is a pretty good deal. Even better this book shows how to objectively measure all of this and pinpoints where to place effort to improve.

Generalities are great but is my unique team covered here?

Most likely your team is covered since any group of people that works together to achieve common objectives is a team. A team is just a collection of team members. There is an enormous diversity among teams considering skills, types of interaction and the duration of the assemblage of the team. In some teams, the members have unique skills. In other teams, the members have largely similar and interchangeable skills. In some teams, the members interact in a highly structured and rigid fashion. In other teams, the members interact in an unpredictable and dynamic fashion. Teams may be assembled for short periods of time. Other teams may be together for years. It is possible to describe at least three general kinds of teams: Partnership, Competitive and Non-competitive.

Sample Team Models

There are many team models that benefit from optimizing team member behaviors. All of these models are covered in this book. For a moment consider these specific types to be our target:

- Partnership Model

In a partnership, all members have equal power, authority and responsibility, e.g. a marriage, a child's play group, a business partnership.

- Competitive Model

  In a competitive team, one group is pitted against another with some notion of winning and losing, e.g. sports like baseball, football and basketball, armies, American business and international governments.

- Non-competitive Model

  The non-competitive team usually provides a service, e.g. federal, state and local governments, the United Way, the Red Cross and international trade organizations like the World Trade Organization.

Leadership

Why is the subject of leadership brought up in a text about getting the most out of teams? Don't the highest performing teams outgrow management?

High performing teams do outgrow their need for traditional management but they never outgrow their need for leadership. Leadership provides a statement of direction and vision of what should be possible at the end of the current rainbow. Teams need this guidance. More to the point, teams thrive on such guidance.

Unfortunately organizational literature and business school curriculum cover a great deal on management but far less on leadership. And most of what is covered does so in isolation and not with regard the impact on the teams involved.

Clearly much more is needed. This text provides a practical answer that is measurable. Further with the ability to measure leadership comes the ability to identify types of leaders and develop specific-to-type recommendations for further growth and improvement.

It is the intent of this text to describe a fairly wide range of leadership skills and capabilities including those implied by David Chaudron, Ph.D. who tells the following story.

"The chiefs of three villages each set out to build a bridge across a wide chasm. If they could build this bridge, the trade that came would enrich the lives of villagers for generations to come.

The first chief told his workers. 'Go forth and work. Do whatever is necessary to build the bridge.' The villagers established a frenzied pace, for this chief abused those workers who did not follow his commands. The first chief boasted to the other two leaders about the speed of his construction. Unfortunately, because no one coordinated these workers' efforts, the bridge was a haphazard collection of nails and boards. It soon collapsed.

The second chief was watching this mess and decided to learn from the first chief's mistakes. She organized her workers into teams and gave them a plan to build a bridge. At first these workers had success and built the bridge straight as an arrow far over the chasm. She now boasted to the two other chiefs about the accomplishments of her workers. Unfortunately the next major storm destroyed the bridge for the chief did not know how to build structural supports. Her workers became discouraged and abandoned their efforts.

The third chief was watching their efforts and decided to learn from the other chiefs' mistakes. He sent his workers to the other villages to learn what they had done and what they had not done. His workers then developed a plan. In their first step they did not build the bridge at all but focused on creating the support columns they would need. When they completed this task they rapidly finished the bridge."

What must a proposal on leadership concern itself with and cover? What is leadership. According to one dictionary[1] here are some of the critical elements of leadership.

---

[1] The American Heritage College Dictionary, Third Edition, 1997, Houghton Mifflin Company, Boston and New York

- It is a position or office of responsibility and power
- It has the capacity or ability to lead by giving guidance and directions
- It is formulated so as to elicit a desired response on followers
- It shows the way by going in advance

This text addresses all these plus the following:

- How do you objectively measure leadership in a way that gives some indication of what needs to be done to improve?

- How does leadership interact with and effect teams?

FAQs

This section takes up frequently asked questions (FAQs) whose answers need to be made clear from the outset.

There are three kinds of FAQs:

- Unique to teams

- Unique to leadership

- Common to both teams and leadership

Unique to Teams

- **What is new here?**

Two things are new: the inside-out approach regarding the skills needed by team members and the leadership skills that foster these teams. Heretofore little has been written on what the team members skills should be and leadership has been addressed in isolation without considering the effect on high performing teams.

- **What do you mean by an inside-out approach to teams?**

  Simply said: we need to take the perspective of a participant, not that of an observer.

  Team members cannot be told how to handle every situation. Inevitably this fix-the-problem approach fails since the team members lack sufficient contextual experience to match a solution to the right problem.

  Trainers like this cookbook approach though because it sells well to leaders. A lot of consulting fees have been earned this way.

  But team members regularly report that there is little transfer from this training to their real world. The training environment might be interesting, entertaining and have good snacks but it is not the real job environment and it is not clear how to apply what was studied.

  The inside-out approach guarantees that the team members' new skills directly apply and are useful in the real world. When the learning takes place in the job environment, transfer is not an issue.

Unique to Leadership

- **What is new here?**

  All previous work on leadership has wandered around the intellectual forest exploring, metaphorically, tree after tree. But where is the "DNA"? This text provides that answer along with practical measurements and theory supporting these conclusions.

- **What do you mean the "DNA"?**

  Leadership can be described from many different directions, as can all behaviors. The great difficulty is to find, if they exist, the most basic leadership behaviors that if mastered allow for the diverse variations needed to confront the complexities of daily business. This text provides these.

In Common

- **If everyone learns how to be a high achieving team member and all the leaders do their part, can everyone have superlative results?**

  Yes, but of course, not everyone is willing to pay the piper. Those who do will benefit and likely benefit disproportionately beyond common expectations. The differences in performance experienced by teams and leaders is not just somewhat better or even one or two times better. Experience has shown that the scale from the beginner to the expert is about one thousand times better. This is an enormous potential payoff. But it does take discipline and commitment.

- **How do you know these skills are the right ones and are comprehensive?**

  Observation and research, available literature, experience, prototyping and actual usage. This approach has not been invented but rather discovered. What is described here has been in front of our eyes but only now organized and validated in current American business and culture.

- **It all sounds too good to be true. Is it?**

  Anything that sounds too good to be true is too good to be true. So too, here, because there is a substantial challenge for the team members individually and collectively, the leader and the greater organization.

Make no mistake. There is a price to be paid. All are being asked to become more sophisticated by learning and using these skills. This takes significant effort and energy, time, patience, insight and self-examination and trust in the process. Not everyone will be up to this task; nor will everyone have the patience and discipline.

- **So, why not just send everyone to class like we've done before?**

Transfer of the classroom learning to the real world is difficult and expensive in both time and money. There is a better way using these skills.

Skills that work in the real job are not easy to learn in a classroom. The classroom encourages a theoretical, conceptual, disconnected-from-the-real-world approach. The classroom is appropriate for some skills but not for those that involve interpersonal interaction.

The best classroom is the actual team in the actual work environment. For example, would it ever do much good to tell a child how to ride a bicycle? One can certainly teach safety and maintenance concepts but to learn how to ride, the child must get on, be protected, and learn by doing. In a like manner, these skills can be rapidly acquired and applied.

- **Why use this material now?**

To compete and stay in business.

The urgency to use this material varies based on how competitive one wants to be. Some strive for high achievement and will be rapid adopters. Others are more resistant to new learnings and will wait to see how the rapid adopters do.

There is no mandatory requirement that any organization use this material. It will depend on the organization's need for early success with high achieving teams. For those who seek this success, these skills are direct answer.

Testimonials

The best people to say whether the approach taken here works are those who have used it. The following are three examples of people and their idiosyncratic experiences. These are not special people with unique capabilities. They are ordinary people like the rest of us. Their particular specialty is in the computer technology business that brought them together as strangers. They then developed into a high performing self-managing team.

Software Development Programmer

When first encountered this programmer was ready to quit the business. She was very angry and depressed about herself, about the computer business and how she fit into the picture. She turned her feelings in on herself and felt nearly empty of self-worth.

But something changed in a major way as a result of her participation and contribution to the team. Here is now where she is.

- "I see myself not as a victim but as a victor now. And the more victorious I become, the more victorious the company becomes.

    ✓ I am validated as a person. The circumstances I have been through are labeled just that: circumstances.

✓ The past does not define the future - there is hope.

✓ There is freedom to choose within the team how work is done and by whom.

✓ There is no competition among the members of the team but only competition within a team member:

> There is the personal challenge to do one's best.

> There are opportunities for each person to stretch and grow.

> Each person feels she has a non-adversarial team, which becomes a safe place from which to operate.

> Our energy is applied to tasks and projects - not for jockeying for position or status or any other political posturing."

How did this complete reversal happen? How long did it take? In reverse order, here are the answers.

- About two years to move from complete defeat to regular high achievement

- By building trust in the team and self, and experiencing significant positive business achievement

This skips over the sometimes teary, angry and frustrating interactions that occurred both privately and publicly in the team. During the process this programmer had a mentor - the manager—who constantly encouraged her and counseled her about her alternatives. The manager provided training in personal skills needed at times but eventually worked himself out of the picture. The most difficult period was at the beginning when this programmer was working from a very small confidence base. But through repeated small personal successes and observing other team members going through some of the same experience, this person made significant headway as can be seen from her report.

Business Planner

Experienced business managers sometimes focus only on business performance, i.e. profit, margin, investment and the like. This experienced business manager believed, initially, he could do his job very well, thank-you, and did not need anyone else. This was a very strong person who did not need or want a team but he found himself in a department where the manager chose to operate the department as a team. Thus the business manager, to keep his job, reluctantly participated. Now let's see what he says:

- "I have sometimes been accused of being a 'green eye shade' type who cares only about business profitability. Well, there is much truth in this. But I also want to know that this profit comes from doing something really useful and not just turning the crank one more turn. I think this new approach works because:

  ✓ It is sound business. The team is constantly measuring itself against real-world forces.

  ✓ The team has no fixed hierarchy.

  ✓ The team depends on the people with the skills that are most needed for the moment. Which, by the way, constantly change.

  ✓ It doesn't require a superman or superwoman."

What turned this independent, non-believer into such a convert? Well in every business plan there are unknowns and unknowables - so called gaps. Usually business planners are required to make sure their plans account for these conditions - but not over account. This is not only difficult to do but also a very, very difficult judgement to make.

This business planner was surprised to find others on his team identifying gaps the business planner had missed and then the team member even filling in these gaps. As the gaps got filled, this was done sometimes without guidance from this business planner. It amazed him that non-business people could perform his specialty and, on a limited basis, do as well. Sometimes, embarrassingly, even better.

When someone covers your "southern exposure" and does not demand anything for it and does not embarrass you then trust is built. There is magic in becoming a high performing team; not just the value of the skills themselves but also the trust and support built among the team members. When trust and realistic self-worth is present, an intimate unselfish collaboration is fostered and becomes the norm. Unsolicited volunteering spontaneously occurs. In this case the business planner became a mentor to the team and taught them more about his specialty. The result was that they understood what he was doing, he knew this and felt appreciated for once and he was motivated to become more flexible and creative in his business alternatives.

Be not misled. This was not just some bland happy family without any troubles. These are real people with all the weaknesses you might expect. But they also came to depend on each other realistically and they became self-managing as a group. Did this pose a problem for the manager? Let's look in on him next.

Manager of Professionals

It would appear that the team members appreciated the new team environment but what about the department manager? How did he react? Did he feel threatened?

- "I went into management for multiple reasons, some idealistic and some more grubby. One reason was because I felt I could do better than most of the managers I had had. Well, the job was harder than I thought until we took this approach. Under the old way, I had too many demands, too much information I had to handle and too little help from either my manager or my department. This new approach has done a lot for me; and has, most important, made my job satisfying beyond even my original hopes and expectations.

  ✓ My department is performing at an outstanding level.

  ✓ The morale is excellent.

  ✓ I feel the department is on my team and I am on theirs.

  ✓ My manager is impressed and views my department's results most favorably. My boss sees me as a leader with greater potential.

  ✓ I get respect from my peers. Some have even asked 'How do you do it?'

This manager went through just as much transformation as the members of his department. This was not easy since the greater organization was and still is very much hierarchically oriented. But the results were amazing—the department did its job in such a superior manner that it revolutionized the business the business group is in, was a technologically innovative leader, and most important profitable. Awards, promotions and other recognitions have followed.

How Teams Work

Teams have three independent processes operating that combine to produce what is perceived as the team performance.

1. Inclusion Process

   This process determines how much capability the team will perceive it has and provides the knowledge and skill resources for the team. Note that as restrictions, limitations and exclusions are imposed either by the team or on the team, then the team operates with less ability and with an increased risk of making ill informed and inappropriate decisions and actions. Inclusion determines the resources available to the team. It is the core material from which the team develops its contributions, actions and results. Obviously if more is included then the potential for more output from the team is enabled; likewise less may produce less.

2. Synergy Process

   This process determines how cooperatively and focused the team will spend its resources allowed by the Inclusion process. If Inclusion is maximized then synergy has much to work with. The synergy process is the mechanism by which the team actually produces results. The Synergy process is strange in that it is not possible to make it happen, i.e. to force it to happen. Synergy is built on trust, motivation and confidence and thus can be disabled but not ensured. To maximize Synergy it is necessary to minimize those factors that would disable it.

3. Integration Into the Greater Organization Process (abbreviated as the Integration Process)

1

Of the results produced by the team, some are taken forward to the greater organization. The Integration Process is the mechanism by which team results are taken forward and become useful to the greater organization. Note that the team skills of Inclusion and Synergy that have been turned inward to the benefit of the team so far, these skills are now used turned outward away from the team during Integration. If the team has become skilled with Inclusion and Synergy, then they have a greater potential for success during Integration.

For Better or Worse

These three processes operate in a self-enhancing or self-reducing manner. When they are self-enhancing they behave like an amplifier; when self-reducing like a filter. The quality of the team member interactions, the way information is used within the team and the type of feedback present all combine to either enhance all team member contributions or stifle them. As team members interact, these amplifications and filterings accumulate and may tend to allow the team to radically improve their results or may tend to frustrate and impede performance previously achieved.

Cascade of Processes

The work products and the team performance are a result of the interaction of these three processes. The output of the team however is not a direct result of each of the individual processes. Rather they combine in a serial fashion and all three have their mutual simultaneous effect on team performance. To summarize, the process interactions work in this fashion.

- The team members bring to the team all sorts of information, capability and potential.

- The Inclusion Process either amplifies or filters the information, capability and potential and the results are the grist for the Synergy Process.

- The Synergy Process operates on information, capability and potential of the team and produces more or fewer results of potential value to the greater organization.

- Finally, the Integration Process delivers the team results to the greater organization, which may perceive these results of more or less value.

Take note of the amplification and/or filtering that occurs in each of these processes and how the output of one process is the input for the next. These are independent processes serially depending on the output of each preceding process. The cascade effect is accumulative and can cause a massive difference between one team who operates low in all processes from another team that operates high in all the processes. Theoretically the difference between these two extremes is a factor of 1000 in performance.

Too it can be predicted with this model that mixed results also occur. For example a team might have a great Inclusion process but a terrible Synergy process, i.e. they just can not figure out what to work on together and do something useful. The results of such a team falls somewhere in-between the extremes and the prescription for such a team would be to improve on their synergy skills.

For the best results, a team needs for all three processes - Inclusion, Synergy and Integration - to be operating as amplifiers simultaneously. This can be quite challenging and is not easily or automatically achieved. Experimental observation has shown that often one of these processes is not well developed and hence we see with most teams less than stellar results and fulfillment of many negative team stereotypes.

So how does a team of strangers come together and scale the heights projected by theory? The obvious and unpleasantly simple answer is to start where you are and then improve. There is no quick fix.

In our Western society which gives significant weight to rules and hierarchy, a team must be guided, trained and lead through the initial rigors of turning the critical processes into amplifiers. Then when a team has achieved an overall midrange performance, the subtle fine-tuning of the interactions of the individuals must become the complete responsibility of the team members alone.

The team must become self-managing and now struggle with performing all the management roles - planning, organizing and controlling - within the team while not only maintaining performance but raising the bar and increasing the useful results. This is a significant mountain to scale and not one that all teams will choose to attack. The surprising thing is that so many teams do try to climb to the peaks and so many actually do make it to the top.

As it turns out, this growth just described is enormously satisfying to the team members. These high achievers report the payoff is always in terms of performance, camaraderie, recognition and appreciation. So we must look beyond the team processes to full understand how this all comes together. Team leadership plays an important role that changes radically as the team sophistication develops. This influence of team leadership will be separately investigated.

Team Skills

Within the three team processes there are nine critical team member skills. Note that it is necessary not only that the skills are expressed but also that other team members perceive these attributes as present. These skills are in a hierarchy; i.e. Listen and Support must be present before and takes priority over Fight Fair.

- Inclusion Process
  1) Listen and Support
  2) Fight Fair
  3) Value the Whole

- Synergy Process
  4) First Things First
  5) Find and Keep Resources Used
  6) Share the Burdens

- Constant Improvement Process
  7) Use the Inclusion and Synergy process skills
  8) Measure, type and develop prescriptions
  9) Obtain outside feedback

Each team member must express these skills and this expression must be voluntary.

Skill 1 - Listen and Support

It sounds so simple to "listen and suppor:". Be neither is so easy. The following quotation, from a poster my mother-in-law displayed prominently, shows what often happens.

> I know that you believe you
> understand what you th nk I said
>
> But
>
> I am not sure you realize that what you
> heard is not what I meant.

In American business some would say that the norm is to talk, sell and argue rather than to listen and much less support. Often the purpose of listening is not to listen but rather to figure

5

out how to convince the other person of your view and turn around what they say into something that can be used for your own purposes. The consequence is that the other person is not really listened to. This interaction can even occur among intimates.

Sometimes in a conversation my wife may concentrate on what she is going to say in response to what I have said, unfortunately to the exclusion of listening any further to what I am saying. She may go so far as to interrupt what I am saying to introduce an unrelated observation or a brand new thought. At times I can handle this. At other times, when I am struggling to develop my own thoughts, the interruption is disruptive to the point that I loose my train of thought and may experience frustration with her and myself. In this intimate relationship with my wife, here is the person who most cares about me, performing an uncaring action, all the while trying to show their caring by interacting. This can be very frustrating for both parties.

Our desire is naturally to be involved in a creative, spontaneous dialog. However when we spend our best efforts figuring out what to say in response to another we may slip into a dual monologue—or a duologue for short. A duologue is two people talking about separate subjects, taking turns in talking but neither is responding to what the other is saying—not really. Is there a way to ensure better communication and not slip into a duologue?

Perfect Communication Theory

Listening and support requires excellent communication. To do so, it is helpful to briefly examine what it takes for perfect communication and examine how it gets fouled up.

The model for perfect communication involves an alternating repeating cycle in which one person takes on the role of communicator and is the source of some new information while the other person takes on the role of receiver and is challenged to understand the ccmmunicator. The repeating cycle has three small steps.

a) Offer of Information
b) Acknowledge Receipt
c) Verify What Was Received Is OK

Take the following everyday interaction as an illustration of how we naturally perform these functions without conscious thought.

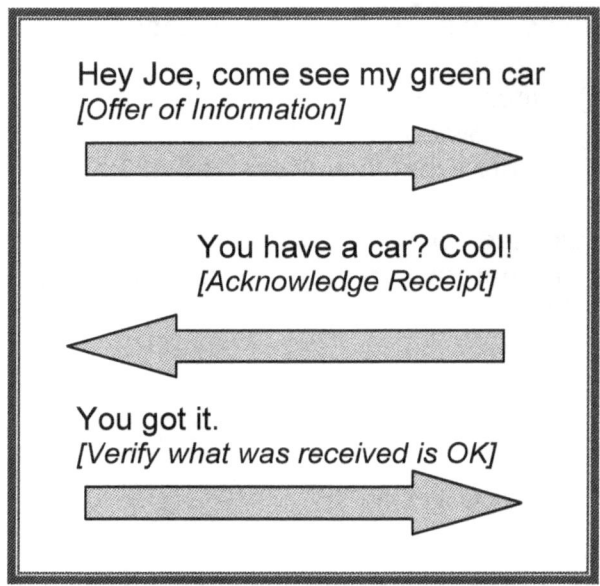

    a) The communicator offered information to Joe about his car.

    b) Joe acknowledged the communicator's information.

    c) The communicator verified Joe got it right.

Perfect communication is:

- Half-duplex

  One must listen while the communicator talks. The communicator is appreciated and respected through this listening.

- Fully acknowledged

  In the course of most conversations, clarity is not automatic. On the contrary, the noise in the listener's head may make it impossible to hear or understand what the communicator is saying. Worse, the receiver may not be consciously aware of attending to the noise. So it is required for the receiver to play back what they think they have heard. This becomes an invitation for the communicator to either correct or verify that the receiver got it right.

- Fully Verified

  The communicator must tell the receiver if they got it right or try to correct what was communicated.

- Alternating

  "Airtime" is the time spent in communicating and it is precious because it is limited. If equal participants communicate, then one expects that both will take up approximately equal amounts of airtime. Alternation ensures this and is easily achieved due to the odd number of steps involved in perfect communication.

  Too, alternation and equal airtime provides a limited, though positive, support for the individuals to each other. Perfect communications, thus, implicitly provides a minimum of both listening and support.

Problems with Communication

To speed up communication we often introduce abbreviations and these, unfortunately, can trip us up. Common problems encountered include:

- Lack of acknowledgement

  The listener has an active role in providing acknowledgement during the communications cycle. Failing that the communicator may drone on and the listener may have all sorts of agendas privately active that do not help.

- Lack of verification

  Verification ensures each communication bit is accurate and can be used to understand what comes next. Failing to verify leaves open whether each bit has been received accurately and this adds to the noise present in subsequent offerings. If the noise builds up enough, the communication can completely break down.

- Minimum or missing alternation

  The use of the receiver as a sounding board is OK so long as the receiver gets what they need. However excessive time spent with one person talking is likely to be perceived to be at the expense of the receiver. Remember that most clinical psychologists, whose job is to listen, limit their sessions to about forty-five minutes.

- Too much information at once

  A gush of information is like drinking information from a fire hose. It is just too much too quick. The way out of this is to prioritize, cover the most important first and slow down. Communications equipment calls this condition data overrun and the solution is to slow down.

- Ambiguity of information

  It is impossible to verify vague points. It is up to the communicator to provide as much clarity as possible and it is up to the receiver to either acknowledge or ask for clarification.

- Rigid enforcement of the communications cycle

  Though the three-step perfect communications cycle guarantees excellent communication, it can also become stilted and mechanical. For teams to work well there needs to be an understanding of the cycle and its appropriate use. Given that sophistication, a more abbreviated free-flowing interchange is more natural since it is backed up with the skills to use the cycle rigidly when it will help.

Skill 2 - Value the Whole

My *American Heritage Dictionary*[2] *defines the whole, in part, as:*

- *"Containing all component parts; complete*
- *No divided or disjointed; in one unit*
- *Constituting the full amount, extent, or duration"*

One might suggest that if you value the whole then you must consider all the team members and what they bring to the table, the content of what the team has been asked to do or provide, and the complete set of customers the team might satisfy.

When you value the whole, you are enriched and empowered to do a more complete job. This is another way to respect the value of the work, you and the team.

When you value the whole, immediately you bump up against the apparently unending diversity of people and their viewpoints. Valuing the whole involves accepting this full scope of the team members and those they deal with and must satisfy.

Skill 3 - Fight Fair

There are no perfect combinations of people to create the perfect team and there is immense, hopefully, diversity. The differences are a rich source of innovative and creative solutions.

---

[2] Houghton-Mifflin, 1982

They also have the potential to generate strong disagreement and argument. Dealing with these possible disagreements needs to be guided by some ground rules rather than being just a melee where the loudest or strongest perseveres.

- Set a time for discussion using the perfect communications cycle

Sometimes disagreements are too important or too difficult to handle spontaneously. Here, a separate meeting can be used to work them out. This allows the team to do its homework and be ready. It allows time for considered thinking. It also allows time for private intra-team discussions that may help.

Beware of trying to negotiate a resolution outside the team. Doing this undermines the team, probably produces a sub-optimal result, may engender cliques and can produce a preeminent issue that has to be dealt with first, i.e. do we have one team or many.

On the other hand, the team may use a subset of the team to do some homework and negotiation for the team. It is essential, however, for these results to be taken back to the team for review and agreement.

- Set aside irrelevant feeling

The issue here is not the elimination of feelings during the argument. Rather the issue is set aside feelings that are no relevant to what is being argued.

A disagreement is more easily resolved if noise is kept out of it and irrelevant feelings add to the noise level. The discussion surrounding the disagreement is not the time to "throw in the kitchen sink".

Personal differences matter but generally should be dealt with one-on-one. At times personal differences cannot be kept out of the team process and they become part of the team process.

Team process is preeminent. The team should deal it with. If it affects the team, the team must deal it with.

- Stick to one issue at a time

    Simplification and clarity are the keys to successful win-win resolutions. Be comprehensive in what may relate but exclude secondary issues. Quite possibly these secondary ones need time too but not now.

- Seek a win-win resolution

    There is a folk song line that goes "Do not muddy the water around us. We may have to drink it soon." The team is the water and whenever any team member "loses", the whole team is hurt. Even though a team member might be wrong about something or a preferred choice is not used for understood reasons, that team member must be cared for. The team needs to ensure that the team member wins even if only through the team winning.

- Use "I" statements rather than "You" statements

    "I" statements take personal responsibility for what you say. They put you out in the open and available for negotiation. In this vulnerable state, it is the time to share the facts as you know them. Remember though, the facts include not just those we all can examine but also include you hunches, feelings and other intangibles. Just take the time to label them for what they are.

- Agree that you can continue the discussion later if you don't make progress now

    Be considerate of your energy and those who disagree with you. Go as far as you can, then try again later. Sometimes a resolution can be had if you just take turns - I will do what you want this time and next time it is my turn.

Sometimes a lack of resolution means that the team should take no action right now.

- Realize that some times are not right for fighting

  There are appropriate times and there are inappropriate times. If there is any doubt about these, the team needs to first discuss and agree on some "rules of the road". This work is preeminent.

- Don't dismiss a disagreement as too trivial.

  Team disagreements are always significant. They may not take much time to resolve but nonetheless are worthy of attention. This goes for non-verbal team disruptions like a member falling asleep.

- Don't bring up subjects or situations that can not be changed.

  The team may share frustrations about how other groups operate or how the business is organized. Constructive discussions within the team to determine how the team is going to deal with these other groups can be constructive. Certainly the team needs to acknowledge the these observations and frustrations even if it is accepted they are unchangeable - at least unchangeable for the time being.

- When you have finished your discussion and are satisfied with the results, document and celebrate.

  All key team activities are worthy of documentation. And team successes, such as a major resolution, are worthy of celebration. Maybe it is just having a cup of coffee together and letting down from the intensity of the negotiation. Though the team's purpose is not social, nonetheless the team has a human need to celebrate and recognize itself.

Skill 4 - First Things First

Teams, like individuals, often succumb to becoming event driven, i.e. the squeaky wheel get the grease. When the team finds itself in this condition, it is clear that the team has not taken the time to prioritize what is most important. To know what is most important, the team must know what the demands and requests are of the team.

The team cannot work on what it does not know exists. It is useful for the team to maintain two action lists:

1) To Do - In Process
   A list of work items which the team is currently working on and making some headway on.

2) To Do - Deferred
   A list of work items which the team acknowledges as demands but for which there is currently no action. Note that the reason for the lack of action should be identified.

Using this approach the team does not just deal with what is being worked on but also acknowledges the additional work that has been requested.

Now the team can evaluate how the requested work items are interconnected. There is an underlying possibility that "Everything is connected." Truer sometimes than others but it is essential information for the team to respond comprehensively. For example, from the interconnections the team may discover the following:

- More than one problem can be solved by one slightly broader solution
- Dependencies force one thing before another
- Bottlenecks appear where multiple activities may be able to work in parallel
- Special skill may need to be acquired
- Similar appearing problems are really different and can be attacked separately

Once the demands and interconnects are sufficiently understood, it is time to prioritize. Prioritization is important but of greater importance is the consensus developed during the discussion generated by the prioritization. It does not matter how the priorities are reached. What matters is that the team now has a sense of what can be done, the urgency and some idea of where to start.

Now the team can plan the work. Some teams plan for a short duration; the development of the plan is quick; and then planning is done again soon. This is common is a software maintenance environment. Other teams have a much longer-term plan. Some have both kinds of plans. It really does not matter so long as it is consistent with the team's way of doing things and there is agreement within the team with the planning duration.

Now it is time to work the plan and by doing so building trust among the team, i.e. we agreed to do it and we did it. But plans should not be done slavishly. When there is good reason to diverge from the plan then the plan should be taken back to the team for update.

And of course then there is the usual chaos. Entropy is the measure of chaos or surprise a team meets and the real world is full of entropy. Physicists tell us that left to its own devices, the real world tends toward entropy. So the encroaching chaos is something the team finds itself regularly pushing back: miscommunication, bad weather, breakage and competition to name a few. Note that team strengths of trust and shared work plans help to reduce entropy.

Skill 5 - Share the Burdens

There is a tendency in American organizations to specialize. When a team needs to take notes then a secretary position is created to handle this activity. This is not sharing the burdens.

Note that the team was put in place to accomplish some critical organizational goals and these did not probably include taking notes. Regardless the team has overhead that must be handled, e.g. note taking, record keeping, updating tracking database (s). The team must handle these overheads such as:

- Leadership.

  Who is going to speak for the team and sit in on other team meetings? Who is going to take the lead to negotiate what the team needs from others?

- Management

  Managers plan, organize and control. Who on the team will do these things?

- Administration

  Who is going to do things like scheduling team meetings, setting the meeting agenda, follow-up on the agenda action items and, as usual, note taking?

- Politics.

  Who is going to advocate for the team needs and compete for team resources and recognition within the greater organization?

- Constant Improvement

  Who is going to ensure the team improves itself, measures where it is as a team and learns from the results?

There is no one way that the burdens can be shared but they must certainly be shared. Certainly the bias toward specialization is one place to start but it is also important that all team members become equally capable, if possible, in all aspects of the team business. Thus, a rigid never changing specialization is not acceptable[3]. But a team might have a secretary for the team for some period and then rotate the assignment.

Skill 6 - Find & Keep Resources Used

Surprisingly teams rarely pay attention to resources other than those they are individually immediately using or planning to use. Thus the team is unaware of:

- What resources are at their disposal collectively
- What resources are secondarily available through other team members
- The overhead and cost of resources
- The life-cycle cost of new resources
- The disposal of unused resources

Teams need to operate on the assumption that everything is out in the open or obvious among the team members. Of course that is not always the case. If you check you own attic, I suspect you will find that there are resources up there you have forgotten about or which you never knew had been put there. So it is with teams.

Hence an early task for any team is to find out what resources the team members have available to them and thus

---

[3] Avoid Hardening of the Team Arteries

My wife and I operate as a small team in our gardening and home maintenance. Though we have developed some specialization of our skills, nonetheless we each at times perform the activities normally performed by the other. This ensures:
- An appreciation of what is involved in the less frequently performed activity
- The ability to operate fully independently and keeps us peers
- Insight so that we can each cooperate and coordinate with the other while they are performing their usual activities
- A sense of fairness
- A sense of making an appreciated contribution

to the team. The place to look to establish this inventory includes:

- The capability of the team members's themselves.
- The physical resources available to the team members.
- The resources the team members have access to through others including the management hierarchy in which team resides.

This inventory is not a one shot deal. It needs to be kept alive and is a key resource to the team. This living inventory can help the team to quickly know what and whom they can call upon.

Once the team knows what resources it has available, it also needs to determine the cost of keeping these resources available. For example, consider the family car expenses.

- Purchase expense

  In 1985, I bought a small sports car called the Toyota MR-2. It cost me about $13,000 new. The same car, in want ads, now sells for around $3,500. The cost cf a new resource is almost always much higher than an older one and the older one might be more reliable since it has gone through the "shake down" or "early life failure."

- Maintenance expense

  My beloved MR-2 gets an oil change every 3,000 miles and other maintenance according to the manufacturer's book. This can be quite expensive but is mandatory to avoid major repairs. So my MR-2 had around 180,000 miles with the original engine and was still going strong when I eventually sold it.

- Usage expense.

I travel about 35 miles to and from work every business day. This takes about 45 minutes one-way and costs me a significant amount for gasoline every year.

- Registration expense

I live in North Carolina and every year for every vehicle we own the state sends us a bill to keep the vehicle registered. I get this bill regardless of how much or how little use the vehicle has.

- Repair expense.

During a recent terrible storm, my doted on MR-2 had an accident. Nothing too serious but it cost $2,000 to get it fixed. When something breaks or is broken, it is fixed.

- Update expense

When I bought the cheapest Nissan truck in 1987, I did not get a rear view mirror with a setting to reduce the glare at night - a so-called day/night mirror. After living with the blinding glare of other cars at night in my ordinary mirror, I went to my friendly Nissan dealer and bought a replacement mirror that did have the day/night feature. It was an update that I wanted. A desired feature.

- Disposal expense

Many years ago, I had a 1949 DeSoto automobile that had the differential completely burn out. The car was an old, worn out hulk. When I disposed of it, it cost me $50 to have it towed to a junkyard. Nothing is free. Even the loss of my only transportation at the time.

The moral of resources is that "there is no free lunch." Resources are valuable if they are used but their lack of use is also costly.

And do not forget the human resources, i.e. people, contacts and the like. Some call it politics but it can also be described as cross team cooperation. And these too will come at an ongoing expense.

Skill 7,8,9 - Constant Improvement

One of the guidelines of Dr. Deming[4] to *"Improve constantly and forever the system of production and service."* Stephen Covey has given us this same admonition[5] in terms of *"Sharpen the Saw."*

None of us is the best they can be when our skills are being acquired or being updated. Even after the acquisition, like the saw, we need to become sharper and better. Some skills are

---

[4] Dr. Edwards Deming was a statistician who became a quality mentor to the Japanese industry after World War II. He died in 1996 but left us a legacy of writings and observations that continue to be most vauable. His 14 points or guidelines include:

- Create constancy of purpose for improvement of product and service
- Adopt the new philosophy
- Cease dependency on mass inspection
- End the practice of awarding business on the price tag alone
- *Improve constantly and forever the system of production and service*
- Institute training
- Institute leadership
- Drive out fear
- Break down barriers between staff areas
- Eliminate slogans, exhortations and targets for the work force
- Eliminate numerical quotas
- Remove barriers to pride of workmanship
- Institute a vigorous program of education and retraining
- Take action to accomplish the transformation

[5] *The Seven Habits of Highly Effective People* by Stephen Covey, Simon and Schuster, 1989

not used often and become unfamiliar; even uncomfortable. Some skills are used over and over and may become mechanical and rigid. We can find ourselves in a rut. All this cries for improvement. Here are some areas for possible continuing update.

7) Team Dynamics and Current Problems

    Real problems that the team encounters, inside the team and outside the team, are the vehicles for constant improvement. If the team can see the immediate value of the team skills as they apply to their current problems then the team may be able to tolerate the time, energy and attention it takes to constantly improve.

8) Team Self-examination and Constant Improvement

    The team needs to take a timeout and observe itself at least twice a year. It is recommended to use the Team Measurement Tool provided in this book. Using this tool, the team can pinpoint which inclusion and synergy skills need further attention. And since it is the team that has made these observations, there is likely less reluctance to do something about them or blame someone from outside the team as not understanding how the team really works.

9) Outside of Team Assessment and Constant Improvement

    Once the team has achieved a high skill level, by their own measurement, and has confidence in itself, then it may be a good time to seek feedback from outside the team. Since the people who can give this feedback are outside the team, only a portion of the questions from the Team Measurement Tool found in this book apply:

- How productive is this team?
- How satisfied are you with the team results?
- How well integrated is this team with the rest of the business?

Depending on the openness and lack of defensiveness of the people giving such feedback, a follow up round table discussion to understand the feedback can be useful. During this session, it is critical that the team uses their "Listen and Support" skills. A measure of the success of this kind of session is if the people giving the feedback come to believe their feedback was heard, was heard accurately and given due consideration, and that future team behaviors are likely to take into account this feedback.

Case Studies

In interaction with teams and their leaders, one comes across a rich mixture of examples of what works, how people see their roles, and the sometimes pressured and frustrating challenges involved. There is a wonderful opportunity to simply watch the performance of individuals in teams and the teams as a group through the insight of the information expounded so far.

Sad to report too that so far more people avoid high performance than enjoy the benefits. This situation appears partly due to the combination of fear on the part of existing management in dealing with virtually any change and practiced powerlessness on the part of employees.

This absence of application of the team skills provides a competitive opportunity for those who would choose to be more competitive and use these theories.

The individual behavior in teams and collective team behavior encountered tends to have repeating patterns. Business administration schools have for some time exercised thinking about such patterns with sample case descriptions. In this manner, the following anecdotal material is offered along with some observations about what is going on and how to deal with it.

These are neither all the possibilities nor even a representative set. These cases are but a teaser and everyone is encouraged to expand on these. We need a continuing exploration of the many possibilities for applying these theories across diverse teams and team leadership found in cultures.

Reluctant Raymond

The situation.

Reluctant Raymond is an experienced programmer. He has taught programming at the college level and is currently moonlighting at the local community college. Reluctant has been with his current employer for about six months, i.e. he is a newcomer. Reluctant is a second generation American Iranian and has a noticeable accent.

Ray recently was assigned to a programming development team working on the next release of an existing product.

At first the team had a great deal of difficulty with Raymond. The team could not get him to perform an assignment on time and produce the needed results. This was very frustrating to the team and pushed Ray into a defensive posture. Some of the team jumped to the conclusion that Ray was not a contributor and wrote Ray off as not a team player. In response Ray has "gotten his back up", become aggressively defensive and become remote from the team.

Not all of the team has written Ray off though. One team member has had private coaching sessions with Raymond where the focus was:

- The team needs Ray.

  Since Ray had been dismissed by some in the team, getting him to believe that the team really needed him was not easy.

- The team is not getting what it needs from Ray

  Ray had decided what the team should need from him and had unilaterally given this to the team. It took some time for Ray to be convinced that the team had a right to set its needs and those were fulfilled by what Ray had offered.

- There are consequences if this situation continues.

  Ray was confronted with the possibility that he could be "fired" from the team. This might not mean leaving the company but it would do harm to Ray's business record. For all involved, it would be best if there could be a positive resolution, i.e. a win-win conclusion.

Ray and the team were at loggerheads for awhile. In time a break through developed. The team member who had been counseling Ray invited the department manager to reaffirm formally what the member had been telling Ray and finally Ray got the message.

- The team needed Ray and was willing to work something out with him.

- Ray discovered he could contribute using his existing skills and without compromising his own values.

It is not entirely clear what finally happened but just like a light switch going on, suddenly Ray and the team were resolved and the work was proceeding not only smoothly but also at a more rapid pace than could have been hoped for. The issues between the team and Ray evaporated. The team, including Ray, were now a well-oiled machine.

By the way, Ray got married during this period.

Reluctant Raymond had a great deal of trouble understanding what the team required. The team tried using their cultural norms. Ray tried based on his cultural background. There was a mismatch and both sides gave up on each other. Probably both sides were confused and frustrated. It takes such an emotional upset sometimes for us to recognize and accept that something new is needed as in this case.

One of the team members, without it being their assignment and without being the team's manager, had insight about what might being going on and took the risk in counseling Ray. Ray rejected the counseling at first and the team mocked the counselor.

The counselor had further insight to involve the department manager to lend formal weight to the confrontation and ensure Ray understood this confrontation could not be left unresolved. Ray now got the message when delivered with this formal emphasis.

Once this issue was resolved, it became evident that more than just this issue was resolved. Many issues were related.

- Ray's relationship with the team.

- The team's skill and capability in dealing with a non-performing member.

- The team's responsibility in dealing with non-performance versus the role of the department manager.

- The freedom of a team member to counsel another and have that counseling supported formally.

Observations

Inclusion is easier to talk about than do. This is especially so when there is a mismatch of norms or values that are ordinary and bedrock like cultural norms. Ray's norm was that a manager had all authority; the team's norm was that the team had almost all authority; and the manager felt he could exercise all authority if needs be.

In American culture there is a tendency to force-fit problems, i.e. if it doesn't fit, force it. When Ray did not perform there was a tendency to ascribe characteristics like uncooperative and uncaring and to want to crush Ray on the part of the team. Fortunately Ray was strong enough to not capitulate and he stood his ground. Unfortunately the confrontation nearly got out of hand since the parties were unaware of the assumptions in their own behavior and the consequences they were generating. Dr. Deming said that of the problems we consider to be the most important and significant we created 85% of these. So it can be seen in this case.

The team member who listened and supported both the team and Ray provided the catalyst for positively resolving this confrontation. The skill of listening and support is extremely powerful and works magic to bring people together. Also the appropriate use of the manager's power to confront Ray with the urgent need for resolution was essential. Effective teams learn where specific skills and powers can be found, how to invoke them when needed, and then appropriately use them.

Post script: Ray became rapidly a team leader himself. He has gone on to lead others and is very successful today.

Angry Andrew

The Situation

Angry Andrew was part of a small team that was expanded in part due to the excellent work of Andrew. Angry Andrew anticipated this and saw himself as the next team leader. Unfortunately this was not to be so.

A different team leader was assigned and Andrew withdrew into his anger about being overlooked and, obviously he thought, unappreciated. In fact, Andrew was not unappreciated but the new team leader was more experienced and capable. The new team leader was a major addition but Andrew was not happy and that was clear to the new team leader.

The new leader started out by holding private sessions with each of the team members including Andrew. Then the leader held a series of team meetings to bring out where the team was going and to get the team members to define how they would contribute. Angry Andrew participated but somewhat reluctantly. Yet Andrew wanted to show his stuff, as usual, and found ways he could make significant contributions.

Most important to Andrew, the new team leader encouraged Andrew's contributions and found ways for the rest of the team to augment these and appreciate these.

Persistence paid off for the team leader and his relationship with Andrew. Over a period of about six months Andrew developed an appreciation for the positive leadership of the new manager. Andrew even discovered himself noticing that the new manager made things happen that Andrew did not know how to do. Respect grew on Andrew's part for the manager.

When the team leader left the team after three years, it was Angry Andrew who proposed and organized a going away party for the manager. Andrew had been won over by the skills of the high performing team and the parallel skills of leading such teams. It had made a personal as well as a business difference in Andrew's life.

Observations

The combination of private listening and support and then the public use of this material, while protecting the anonymity of the source, allowed for win-win negotiations among team members and leadership. Once more listening and support skills were critical in bringing together warring camps and setting the stage for major accomplishments.

Andrew was clearly won over by the positive achievements of the team and of the team leader who Andrew gave credit for making this happen. Results mattered to Andrew and the team leader agreed. Results always matter and are the greatest ally in teaching the new skills and of engaging the participants positively.

Another positive element that won over Andrew was the egalitarian aspects of the team skills and in particular "Sharing the Burdens". Andrew was used to working in a specialized hierarchy and expected the dirty work to go to underlings - of which Andrew was not. As the dirty work got spread around, Andrew came to respect not only the team leader but also the other team members.

For most people, high performance is a desirable result however they just have great doubt it can occur here. One thing to emphasize early on are many small successes. This occurred for Angry Andrew. It is a bit like Chinese water torture wearing down doubt, cynicism, anger, frustration and hesitation.[6] Most team members bring a lot of "baggage" with them that took years to accumulate and is not easily given up. Success breeds more success and changes the expectations from negative to positive.

---

[6] Note that the effects of the "Self-fulfilling prophecy" works against the team seeing successes early in the team development while later, after many successes this phenomena works in favor of further growth.

Frightened Fred

The Situation

Frightened Fred desperately wanted to recover his career and reputation. Fred had been demoted and just finished with an ugly divorce. Fred was a frazzle. But Fred would try anything. It just was likely that with his fear and lack of current skills, Fred would make a botch of whatever he touched.

Fred was assigned to a team in which none of the team members had overlapping or common skills. They all mostly worked in parallel with each other. But the department manager was willing to try to us the team member and leader skills described in this book. So the manager met privately with Fred to listen to what Fred wanted to do with his career. The manager also publicly counseled Fred and other member of the team about the details of their work. The manager was an active trainer.

As Frightened Fred had successes, the manager recognized them publicly. Too the manager encouraged the team members to also recognize each other's accomplishments. Sometimes it was just a simple "Thank you."

Slowly Fred blossomed and then suddenly Fred began to display leadership skills too. Fred had known he had these capabilities but his exhaustion and fear had kept these skills in check. Quickly now the manager came to depend on Fred as an alternate team leader. This was a leader "elected" by the team based on performance and not as a formal assignment. Fred's leadership was just accepted and obvious.

Fred was no longer frightened. Fred had healed and in such a manner as to be a major asset to the team and the manager.

Observations

The manager listened to Fred, gave him opportunities that were supported, allowed "baby steps" to be appropriately recognized and got out of the way when Fred progressed to giant steps. The manager's leadership came out in terms of facilitation and training and Fred responded positively.

It is remarkable how rapidly the application of the team and team leader skills creates turnarounds. Fred really was disabled and frightened. It looked like he was lost and the business would not have a strong participant for a long time. Some businesses would probably have fired Fred. Just not a good bet. But as we have seen, the business would have lost a major contributor if it had taken that route. Fred needed leadership and an opportunity to find his own skills and use them.

The use of team and team leader skills also involves teaching these skills both by living them as well as more formally. As this is done the skills and capabilities spread out into other areas of the business unless, of course, there is active punishment for such behaviors.

Punishment? How strange but it is commonplace. The single most supportive act current management can do is to not inflict pain on those growing in these skills. Encouragement is great but as Ted Turner is noted for saying - "Lead, follow or get out of the way".

Disabled Dan

The Situation

In another team one of the team members was a long time employee of the firm. An old timer. Trouble was, Disabled Dan had been told by manager after manager that he was not doing well, probably could not do well, and that this was just not satisfactory.

Dan had come to believe - had been trained to believe - that he could do nothing right. Dan had stopped trying as a result.

He was a basket case ready to be discarded by the business.[7] Dan was used up and ready for the trash heap. Not much could be done with Dan from here.

However Dan's new team leader just didn't buy all this. The new team leader really needed Dan and his skills. There was no one else available to the team. The mother of necessity dipped her hand into their lives.

The team leader at this time was learning about the team and team leader skills. She was going through intensive coaching and counseling from an outside consultant. These new learnings were uncertain but offered hope for dealing with folks like Disabled Dan so the team leader thought she would have a go at Dan with her new skills. It was a situation much like the teacher who reads the lesson the night before teaching it.

The team leader was able to pull it off. Dan was in such great need of being listened to and supported that it was not really too difficult. The team leader and Dan grew during this period very rapidly.

Dan began to believe in himself due to the belief offered by the team leader. It took time and the process was incremental. Before long, other team members began to ask the opinion of Dan, much to his surprise. The whole process was slowly infectious - realistic trust, desire to produce, encouragement to try, and recognition from people that you respect.

Dan exceeded his own experience and gained skills he never expected he could acquire. He no longer was a victim in the business and this spilled over into his person life. He had a history but these were just facts now. He had transcended his background and once again an individual had grown in team skills and gone on to share these with others both inside and outside the team.

To this day, Dan has an optimistic positive outlook and a sense of control. This even in the context of an employer who has been downsizing. Dan has survived layoffs and anticipates

---

[7] It is amazing how often a person is dropped by a business only to be hired into a similar business and do very well. When a business drops someone it does not reflect well on either.

a bright future. He is secure in his team member skills that are highly marketable whether with his current employer or some future one.

Observations

Businesses at times use people up and then discard them. There is an impact to self-worth when a person is laid off. A key part of adult life is woven into career, vocation or job. If this goes well, it can give us confidence that may be transferable to other areas of our lives. When it goes poorly, it can drag us down.

The team member skills provide realistic affirmation of the team member's practical accomplishments and by doing so raises the probability that future achievements may even be better. Success and recognition by those who know your work most intimately provide the greatest satisfaction. And satisfaction is a motivator to do it again.

Successful businesses depend on successful employees. If there are employee performance problems, then the business has a vested interest in finding ways to make its employees successful. Discarding people or even working in that direction should be suspect. It is a symptom of managerial failure and not an employee problem. Disabled Dan was a casualty of this kind of business experience.[8] For some who view business as a form of war, then casualties are to be expected and accepted. However take note that these businesses are not sustainable.

Businesses that are built to last find ways to rejuvenate their employees that get hurt. This is especially true if it was the business that did the hurting.

The team member skills are life-giving behaviors that build people rather than tear them down. The skills are not easy to gain and require discipline to implement but they are satisfying

---

[8] It should be noted that sometimes being fired is the best thing that can happen so that the individual is now freed to find more meaningful and satisfying employment. Leaving a bad employer is not all bad.

and successful. Hopefully that is sufficient motivator to stick with them.

Rudderless Robert

The Situation

Robert is a manager of several teams and Robert loves to crow about how well his teams are performing. Would that it was true. Actually ol' Rudderless is just a big political windbag. His crowing is a way of saying, "Look at me and how well I am doing."

Recently Robert agreed for one of his teams to be surveyed. Since Robert was so proud of how well the team was doing, his expectation was that the survey would confirm this expectation. The survey was taken by the team one week and the next week the results were fed back. Since the results were 2 out of 10, the consultant was a bit concerned about a negative reaction from the team

The team response was far more encouraging. After the consultant finished with the feedback, the team spontaneously applauded and one team member commented "Finally someone understands!" A pleasant surprise for the consultant and, clearly, the team.

The results were then discussed with Rudderless but the reaction was quite different. Ol' R.R. understood what the team had said and recognized that they had seen through his sham. The facts did not support his bloated view of himself.

Observations

All is not success. There are those who do not want the truth out in the open. There are those who do not care about high performance and there are more than you might expect. American business has been run from the top-down for a very long time giving many the chance to become comfortable with blaming others and crowing about how wonderful they are. The great majority of these are in middle management.

Leaders have been without a way to measure team and leadership performance in an objective fashion. This was always "soft stuff" that was an art. This is no longer true. Using the approach defined in this book these problems are now solved.

It is also clear that if teams do not progress it is due to negligence on the part of their leaders. Too if the team regresses it reflects on management's actions. Left to their own ends, teams will always try to get better since that is the direction of greatest satisfaction and sense of accomplishment.

Five steps need to take place in an organization to gain experience and confidence with these team skills.

- Survey First

    First a baseline of where the team and leader are operating needs to be established. This is the point to measure future performance against.

- Improve

    Training, appropriate realistic public praise, counseling, and encouragement must take place over time. Time is needed to integrate the learnings and to achieve accomplishments.

- Survey Again

    Are we better off? By how much? Where are our greatest weaknesses now?

- Do the process again

- Correlate Survey to Business Measurements

If the business can understand how the team performance relates to traditional business measurements there is greater hope that the teams will receive sustained support. Using this correlation, the business can now predict the expected improvements as the teams move toward self-management.

Bigger-fish Francine

The Situation

Bigger-fish Francine is a General Manager in a major business. Her focus is profitability and expense reduction. Lots of revenue and layoff the worn out workers first.

Francine is a corporate bully. Beat the employees into submission. In years gone by, a male bully held her job. Now it is a female. Equal opportunity.

Bigger-fish has a major set of problems that she is struggling to solve. She needs more revenue to placate her boss so she is mercilessly attacking the marketing organization demanding that they do a better job. Francine is powerful - very smart and ruthless. Marketing is in trouble and trying to respond to her demands. Of course they can never fulfill these demands. Whenever they make some headway, the demands just get bigger.

Francine knows how to cut expenses. She has done two layoffs in as many years. Since her products are not keeping up with the market evolution, she will probably do another layoff soon. So what if some of these people are the muscle of her organization. The young people she is hiring will make it up with more hours of work per day.

Ol' Bigger-fish was recently given a presentation by a person from her Human Resources (HR) department proposing experimenting with team skills and leadership in a couple of departments to see if this would help Francine's business. But Francine has, as you might guess, bigger fish to fry. Further, why should she believe anything HR has to say anyhow? HR doesn't produce any revenue. If they want to help they should go negotiate better terms from their insurance carrier.

So Bigger-fish Francine is going to continue her aggressive, repressive, bludgeoning approach to "her" business. And her people will continue to be used up and discarded. As long as Bigger-fish is not disciplined, she will continue to abuse everyone below her while at the same time bemoan to confidants that she is the victim. For rest assured that Francine is not happy either.

Observations

Bigger-fish Francines only exist due to the tolerance of higher level executives including, for example, the board of directors. Since Francine's leadership behaviors maintain satisfactory financial results, the superiors tolerate her in the belief that the results justify the means.

Of course this is not sustainable. Exploitation becomes known for what it is and there is always a swing of the pendulum the other way. Unfortunately Francine may never get personally caught unless someone in the hierarchy notices that there is a better way. The top-level leaders that care about building a business that lasts must discipline the Francines of this world. In particular, when the surveys consistently point to Integration problems, then the focus should shift to the superior manager. Only management can fix integration problems.

Timid Team

The Situation

The Timid Team consists of eight people who have an average of about three years with the company. Enough time to lose their new-hire aggressive ambition and enough time to learn passivity. The Timid Team members are afraid of many things.

- Hurting their career growth

- Showing their ignorance

- Expressing their frustration and being too emotional

- Getting out of line with the business

The Timid Team is doing the best it can - not too good but not too bad either. They recently found on the Human Resources internet page references to team and team leadership skills. The team has now taken the survey and invited a HR person to analyze the results and recommend actions.

In all three areas of the survey, the Timid Team came out in the midrange. The HR consultant recommended that the team focuses their efforts on inclusion first, then synergy and last integration. But the Timid Team is having a difficult time making a decision. For now, they are just mildly dissatisfied and planning to continue doing pretty much what they have been doing.

Observations

The Timid Team knows they are skating on thin ice but they are afraid of sticking out their collective necks. It is obvious that the Timid Team needs support and reassurance; that they need to takes some risk but not by themselves.

The HR rep's recommendation is right on the money. The team needs to do what it can first but the team also needs some organizational support.

For leadership, the Timid Team is an opportunity waiting to happen. This group is ready to do better but needs their fears reduced. This is a job for management intervention.

Fragmented Team

The Situation

The Fragmented Team can be described as a team that is team only by name. The Fragmented Team is a group of team leaders on a large project. They are fragmented because they do not work closely with each other even though the project requires a complex integration of a number of technologies.

The Fragmented Team is operating as a disjoint collection of individuals. They meet but do not really communicate. Nor do they want to. Nor are they trying to solve this condition.

The team leader believes this is the best that can be done under the circumstances and he is not trying to make any changes; just survive.

The Fragmented Team is a "train wreck" in the making. Obviously if they continue down this path, the results are going to be disastrous - and there will be no time left in the project since the most severe problems will occur at the end of the project.

Observations

There are two key problems here:

- The team leader is into heavy denial about the consequences of this fragmented team working on an integrated project. This mismatch just will not work.
- The team is tolerating a set of behaviors that could possibly put them out of business, i.e. it is self-destructive. Possibly there is a view that the first team member to "blink" will get all the blame so why be the first.

As usual the right starting point is going to be listen and support. But in addition, the leadership needs to become aware of the disastrous choices the team has made for itself and reverse these. Reversal will take an understanding of why the team members are afraid to take any corrective action not just demanding that they do something else.

Most large projects have reviews and audits. In the past these activities covered mainly the technical aspects of the future. In the future it would be good business to also include surveys of the major teams and appropriate action plans based on these results. For the Fragmented Team this would result in training in inclusion skills.

Doing-well Team

The Situation

You do win some but these too can pose problems. Suppose a team measures out an 8 on a scale of 10. Might this team become self-satisfied and not challenge themselves any further?

Observations

If the leadership allows the team to stop surveys and improvements, the leadership is missing an obvious dynamic - why is the team doing this? Most likely the manager is creating conditions that the team is simply adapting to. The solution is to ask the team for their reasoning.

Note that it is not possible for a team to stand still. If they become passive and self-satisfied they will regress.

In this situation there are two actions immediately advised:

- Get the manager on the team

The manager is not competent who does not know what is going on in and with the team. The solution is for the manager to begin working inside the team.

There is a risk here in that if the manager has not worked well with the team for some time, their presence in the team will slow down the team processes radically. If this happens, superior management must decide if the team leader is the right one for the investment that must be made. Regardless whoever is the team leader must operate as part of the team.

Survey the team and work on the weakest skills first

The team knows it can improve. Survey the team so that what the team already knows becomes public to the team and their leadership. Then take action to improve the weakest skill first and/or obtain a more qualified leader.

Measurement & Interpretation

In order for team member performance to improve, there needs to be a means for feedback to these individuals and a consistent approach to the interpretation of this feedback. To develop the necessary feedback, the most direct approach is taken - ask the principles involved and those who are dependent on them and interact with them.

There are no right or wrong, good or bad responses to the questionnaire. The emphasis is on the state of the performance of the team and how that performance is perceived outside the team. The responses are on a ten-point scale where 1 means the minimum or least result and 10 means the greatest or maximum result **reasonably**[9] conceivable. If there is no discernable performance on an item then it should be reported

[9] Reasonably conceivable does not mean an idealistic unattainable dream. There must be some rationale, some reason to believe that more can be achieved on the scale. It is critical that a "10" can be achieved.

as zero. Too, if the question does not apply or the reporter has no opinion then the response should be left blank.

In this section, we will define the team performance questionnaire, when to use and what to do with the information obtained, i.e. appropriate follow up prescriptions and actions.

Questionnaire

The team member questionnaire is administered to the team members and a subset optionally to the team's management and others who depend on or are affected by the performance of the team.

There are two sets of questions in the team member questionnaire[10]. All questions are used with the team members but only the questions taking an outside view of the team are used with team management and others.

- Questions taking the view from outside the team.
    - ✓ How productive is this team?
    - ✓ How satisfied are you with the team results?
    - ✓ How well integrated is the team with the greater organization?

- Questions taking the view from inside the team.
    - ✓ How well does the team listen and support its members?
    - ✓ How well does the team value the whole?
    - ✓ How well does the team fight fair?
    - ✓ How well does the team put first things first?
    - ✓ How well does the team share the burdens?
    - ✓ How well does the team find and keep resources it uses?
    - ✓ How well does the team constantly improve?

---

[10] See appendix A for the actual questionnaire.

Scoring

The team member questionnaire is scored separately[11] for the team members from questionnaires from team managers and leaders and others outside the team.

- Each question is separately averaged across all the responses.

- The first three question responses are then averaged. This is the **Integration** score (a value between 0 and 10). If the value is between 0 and 5, the Integration score is recorded as **Low**; otherwise it is recorded as **High**.

- This completes the scoring for responses from those outside the team.

- The second three question responses are then averaged. This is the **Inclusion** score (a value between 0 and 10). If the value is between 0 and 5, the Inclusion score is recorded as **Low**; otherwise it is recorded as **High**.

- The third three question responses are then averaged. This is the **Synergy** score (a value between 0 and 10). If the value is between 0 and 5, the Synergy score is recorded as **Low**; otherwise it is recorded as **High**.

- The three averages (Inclusion, Synergy and Integration) are multiplied together and the result divided by 100 resulting in an **Overall** score (a value between 0 and 10).

- Last, the responses to the tenth question, "How well does the team constantly improve?" is averaged. This is the **Improvement** score (a value between 0 and 10). If the value is between 0 and 5, the Improvement is recorded as **Weak**; otherwise it is recorded as **Strong**.

---

[11] See Appendix B for Scoring Worksheet and Team Summary Report forms.

Inclusion	Synergy	Integ.	*Type of team*
L	L	L	Bureaucracy
L	L	H	Task Force
L	H	L	Loose Cannon Individuals
H	L	L	Country Club
L	H	H	Familiar Individuals
H	L	H	New Team
H	H	L	Breakaway Loose Cannon Group
H	H	H	Self-managing

The integration score of management and others outside the team is used as a sanity check; i.e. to verify that the team's perception of itself within the greater organization is congruent with the greater organization's perception of the team. So long as the team and the organization are close (within two points of each other), the team score is used. When the team assessment differs by more than two points with the greater organization, then the lesser of the two assessments is used.

Types

There are eight profiles of teams based on their inclusion, synergy and integration scores measured as low or high. Each of these combinations produces a particular type of team that will be further described.

Types Defined

Let's take a moment to understand each of these team types.

• Bureaucracy.

This type is low in all aspects of team activity. These teams are perceived as doing little of value including having an assignment of no great importance. These teams produce little, consume resources and often have unhappy team members.

- Task Force.

  This type is a group of strangers that have been thrown together for an important task. The organization wants an answer and is anxious to hear what the team has to say. These teams are expected to produce quickly and have unpredictable team member relationships.

- Loose Cannon Individuals.

  This is a group of strong individuals who don't see much use in being on a team. These folks have little relationship with each other though individually they can be quite productive. As a result, the individuals in the team may ignore what the team was put in place to do and go their own merry way doing other things.

- Country Club.

  This is a group of friends who pay more attention to caring for each other than in getting any important business done. This type is focused on their relationship and little on the business needs.

- Familiar Individuals.

  This type describes most management teams where the viewpoint is "If you want to push for something you can probably get it done but no one is going to help you very much." This group knows how to get along with each other sufficiently to produce results.

- New Team.

  This type describes members of most business departments where the people don't work directly with each other on a daily basis but rather work mostly in parallel with each other. Most business departments never get past this profile since the cooperation, collaboration and mutual support among the team members is not developed.

- Breakaway Loose Cannon Group

  This type can perform at a very high level and may produce excellent business results but these results are not needed, appreciated or used by the greater organization. Since this type is thus a small business of its own, there may build a strong desire on the part of these team members to leave the greater organization and strike out on their own. This is the group that produces so-called "Spin offs".

- Self-managing.

  This type is self-motivated, contributing to the greater organization in a positive manner and able to adjust, adapt and improve as needs be. This type has reached the stage where traditional hierarchical management is no longer either appropriate or helpful.

Prescriptions

Team development requires organization management intervention for all teams. Practical managers usually ask for a roadmap to tell them what actions should be taken. Given the diversity of teams such a roadmap must be general purpose. Here is such a simple roadmap:

1. Ask the team to assess themselves and report where they are.
2. Recognize that management decision and action is required to deal with issues of integration.
3. Recognize that some teams should go away.
4. Train the team consistent with their reported type.
5. Give time for the team to incorporate the new learnings into their performance.
6. Do this roadmap again.

There are predictable appropriate choices and interventions based on team type. The choices and prescriptions center on mostly training though other alternatives are offered.

Team Type	Prescription/Choices
Bureaucracy	1. Eliminate team and assign people to useful activities or teams 2. Provide team with valued assignment 3. Train the team in inclusion skills 4. Train team in synergy skills.
Task Force	1. Train the team in inclusion skills 2. Train the team in synergy skills
Loose Cannons Individuals	1. Eliminate team and let individuals work alone 2. Provide team with valued assignment 3. Train the team in inclusion skills.
Country Club	1. Eliminate team and assign people to useful activities or teams. 2. Provide team with valued assignment 3. Train the team in synergy skills.
Familiar Individuals	1. Train the team in inclusion skills 2. Show the team the potential for outstanding results and their interdependency on each other to accomplish this. 3. Provide team feedback from peers and superiors.
New Team	1. Train the team in synergy skills.
Breakaway Loose Cannons	1. Eliminate team and assign people to useful activities or teams. 2. Provide team feedback from peers and superiors. 3. Provide team with valued assignment

Self-managing	1. Train team on weakest skill.
	2. Provide team feedback from peers and superiors.
	3. Provide access of team to situations where superiors expose their business needs.
	4. Expand team responsibilities.

How Leadership Works

Leaders have three independent processes operating that combine to produce what is perceived as excellence in leadership.

1. Build Trust Process

    By definition a leader is somehow ahead of those he would lead - if not physically or technically then intellectually or with insight. But a leader is nothing if no one follows and getting others to follow voluntarily involves trust.

    Trust is taken to the ability of the leader to instill in subordinates the belief in a future state that can be achieved and is desirable. Too, trust has an element of history, i.e. that this leader previously delivered what was promised so there is a basis to believe this leader will do so again.

    Leadership absolutely depends on trust and without trust there is no leadership. There is slavery where through some element of force people can be pushed along but note that when the leader is pushing they cannot be leading.

2. Use Strength Process

    A leader must find ways for his people to do something useful and competitive. The leader must setup a set of values and principles that when followed will achieve a useful expenditure for both subordinates and greater organization.

3. Integration Into the Greater Organization Process

    Of the results produced by the leader's organization elements, some are used by the greater organization and some fall by the wayside. The integration process is the mechanism by which the leader optimizes what gets used.

For Better or Worse

These three processes operate in a self-enhancing or self-defeating manner. All of the interactions of the leader and his organization combine to either amplify the effectiveness of the leader and his organization, or to filter out the potential of this combination. These three processes operate as if they were connected in a serial fashion:

- The subordinates bring to the leader varying degrees of trust and knowledge of what is required by the leader. The leader either builds up this trust or consumes it and what is left is the good faith and energy that is the strength of the leader's organization.

- The leader's organization strength can be turned to many purposes, not all of which are valuable to the greater organization. And some the leader's organization strength needs to be spent on that organization. Just like an individual spends around eleven hours a day in rest and eating, so too an organization must tend to its own needs.

- Finally, the Integration process operates on the results of the leader's organization and the greater organization may perceive a large or small contribution.

Cascade of Processes

Amplification and/or filtering occur in each of these processes.

Also the output of one process is the input for the next. Though they are independent processes, they serially depend on each other. The cascade effect is accumulative and can cause a massive difference from one leader who operates low in all processes to another leader operating high in all processes. Theoretically the difference between these tow extremes is a factor of 1000 in performance.

Too it can be observed that with this theoretical model that mixed results also occur. For example a leader may have a great Build Trust process but a terrible Use Strength process, i.e. they just can not figure how to get their people working together constructively. The results of such leadership are that it falls in-between the extremes and the prescription for such leadership would be to improve their Use Strength skills.

For the best results, a leader needs for all three processes - Build Trust, Use Strength and Integration - to be operating as amplifiers simultaneously. This is challenging and is not easily or automatically achieved. Experimental observation has shown that often one of these processes is not well developed and hence we see with most leaders less than stellar results and fulfillment of many negative stereotypes.

So how does a leader go about scaling the heights projected by theory? The obvious and unpleasantly simple answer is to start with where you are and then improve. There is no quick fix.

In our Western cowboy-mentality there is the expectation that leaders will be self-made and some are up to a point. The fantasy is that a leader appears fully formed. The reality is otherwise.

Initially, leaders are developed through coaching, counseling and mentoring by other leaders. When a leader has achieved midrange performance as a leader, then things really become more demanding.

World-class leaders require subtle fine-tuning of their leadership skills that can only be done over some time. So why would someone choose this career path?

Leadership has big payoffs in money, power and prestige. But there are an even bigger payoffs for world-class leadership.

Those who have achieved a degree of these levels are more personally confident while displaying greater humility than they had to start with. There is enormous personal satisfaction in the accomplishment including awareness of the leader's contribution to well being of others. All who have tried and achieved these levels report it as the greatest time in their lives.

Leadership Skills

There are skills that provide leadership to both the creation and maintenance of high achieving teams. Dr. Deming gave us his 14 Points. Also, *Built To Last*[12] explores the stock market measurable effects of different leadership values. From this in part, it is clear the following leadership skills are always valuable to the organization but are essential to the creation and maintenance of high achieving teams. Said another way, without these leadership values and behaviors, high achieving teams will come and go but they will never have a sustained life or contribution to the organization. Note these skills are in a hierarchy; i.e. Walk Like You Talk must be present before and takes priority over Reduce Fear.

- Build Trust Process
  (a) Walk Like You Talk
  (b) Reduce Fear
  (c) Accept Only Win-Win Contracts

- Use The Trust Process
  (d) Increase Feedback
  (e) Constancy of Purpose
  (f) Define organization principles, sell and administer

- Constant Improvement
  g) Use the Build Trust and Use Trust process skills
  h) Measure, type and develop prescriptions
  i) Obtain outside feedback

---

[12] *Built To last - Successful Habits of Visionary Companies*, James C. Collins and Jerry I. Porras, Harper Business, 1994

Skill A - Walk Like You Talk

The leader must put action ahead of rhetoric. Though rhetoric can be useful by providing a rational explanation of what the leader is trying to do and how she hopes to accomplish these results, rhetoric without commensurate action communicates a message of manipulation. Worse, this message, since it comes from the leader, implies that manipulation is not only OK but considered a proper technique for getting things done. By the way, manipulation is never welcome by subordinates since it is a disrespectful and demeaning form of control.

Some leaders cannot get past this skill since they are not good with words. For these leaders the advice is to say less and let their actions speak for them. Actions always speak louder than words and words can never, never undo what actions have done. Yes, you can fool some of the people all of the time but even ordinary people are quite perceptive and, in time, see through such a con game. And, of course, if it was OK for the leader to con the team then this same value works up the organization too. Such leaders find they are receiving unreliable information and for the life of them cannot figure out how to solve the problem.

A second use of words and rhetoric is that it projects results in the future, i.e. before there is enough time and history of results to state the same thing. Thus the leader's rhetoric may provide leadership beyond what the leader can immediately do. Words point the way.

Unfortunately, if the rhetoric and the future results do not match, the team will feel misled.

Matching how you walk with how you talk increases the trust that the team has that the future will turn out the way the leader has said it will. If the words and the results match then trust is increased; if the words and results do not match then trust is reduced.

And for a leader, the coin of the realm is trust. It is like money in the bank. The more the leader is trusted then the more options and choices the leader has.

Skill B - Reduce Fear

Fear might not be among the first things you would comment on about an organization but fear is the single-greatest cause of poor performance in organizations.

Fear is sometimes an inadvertent result of the leader's choices, sometimes imposed on the business by outside forces, and sometimes an intentional mechanism used by leaders to maintain the leader's sense of control and personal power.

When fear is present it consumes the team members' time and energy. But remember that there is always a limit on the team members' time and energy and if it is spent on fear or responding to this fear, then it is not being spent on doing something useful

Fear also has unintended side effects - people have a tendency to give as good as they get, i.e. an eye for an eye. Last, the fearful person has three choices: fight, flight or confront and none of these is particularly attractive.

Confrontation is often not chosen due to the difference in power between the leader and the team members. Remember that insubordination remains an accepted reason for firing someone.

Flight implies hiding somehow or, more likely, leaving the leader's organization, i.e. bailing out of the ship. Since most people need a continuing income and movement within or among organizations takes time, even when this alternative is chosen it has significant time delays built-in.

Fight is the most frequent response people choose in the form of passive aggression. Basically the fearful person kowtows to the leader, may even agree publicly, but then goes on to undermine what the leader wants, possibly at the expense of themselves and their team. It is a way of getting "even." You hurt me so I will hurt you. And the greater the perception of the hurt inflicted, then the greater the motivation to return the insult. It may explain the aberrant aggressive behavior known as "going postal."

However, there are conditions where leaders find that fear accomplishes what they want in the short term - no open disagreement, immediate conformance and no creativity or new ways to approach the situation. Parents find themselves doing this when they shout at their children to stay out of the roadway. The parents will turn their own fear into having the child experiencing fear too. And, it must be said, there may be an appropriate time and place for these actions on the part of the leader. But it should be remembered that instilling fear reduces trust.

Controlling through fear, though common, destroys the team's ability to not only trust the leader but also to trust themselves. Instilling fear is a way to say to the team that the leader knows best and thus the team is not competent to make such decisions. This is an effective way to disable the team and reduce its effectiveness.

Skill C - Accept Only Win-Win Contracts

American business has never been built on win-win contracts alone. American business is competitive with strong notions of winners and losers. We have taken a competitive sports model and inappropriately applied it to our businesses. If one business wins then the other business loses. Why would anyone knowingly enter into such a contract?

The reality is that most contracts are sort-of-win—sort-of-win. But it turns out that a win-win relationship is optimal for all parties and, guess what, builds even further trust. Let's look at how a win-win negotiation helps both parties.

- Both parties are stronger

  By definition, a win-win contract means that both parties benefit to an equivalent degree - though usually not in identical ways. As a result, both parties are stronger by having gained significantly and appropriately to each party. The contract does not deplete either but rather enhances both.

- Both parties become equals

  For example, American manufacturing has learned to negotiate just-in-time supplier contracts so that the manufacturer does not need to mainta n a warehouse of parts. Sometimes the manufacturer has had to train the supplier and then assist the supplier in setting up facilities. Sometimes the supplier negotiates with the manufacturer for changes they can make to improve the overall results. Regardless, after the contract, the two parties are equals in areas covered by the contract. Further, the two parties become like a married couple - dependent on each other and stronger for that interdependency.

- Both parties have a realistic basis for trust

  Win-win contracts only work when the parties can realistically trust each other to perform as agreed. And this success can lead to innovation, the opportunity for greater trust and a more interdependent, mutually supportive relationship in the future.

- Both parties are more able participants in expanded future contracts

  Since both parties are stronger, most trustworthy and more trusting; they are prepared to be more capable and, possibly, better partners in the future. The win-win contract builds both and foretells a bright future to the relationship.

Win-win contracts, both inside the orgarization and outside, are the only sustainable basis for high performance among these groups.

Skill D - Increase Feedback

Part of the stockade mentality of some leaders is to seek to have those around who will tell them what they want to hear. Often this condition develops slowly and without conscious awareness of the leader due to information overload[13] that is inherent in a hierarchical organization. The leader may demand that their staff provide only the "net-net" of all situations. In so doing, the leader maintains their focus and direction albeit by denying and ignoring possibly critical information.

Leaders need information to make decisions since a lot rides usually on these decisions. It is difficult to sort through all the information that flows to the leader and as information overload occurs, the leader may begin to shutdown what they see as extraneous input. This approach may work well as a tactic but becomes detrimental if it becomes part of the organization's normal procedures.

The solution is to increase feedback in the organization - both inside the organization as well from outside the organization. Feedback allows timely critical information to get through when most needed and ensures the leader remains in touch with the real world. Clearly those who have a better contact with the real world, and not just what is in their head, have the opportunity to more realistically respond to the real world and be proactive. Those who play ostrich and live in the 52nd State - the state of denial - only manipulate themselves and those they lead into unnecessary and, often, unpleasant situations.

Now this increased feedback can get out of hand if it is just an increase in the noise level of the organization and an opportunity for playing more politics. To manage this increased

---

[13] In hierarchical organizations information is funneled up and there is a risk that this funneling can overload the receiving managers.

information the leader needs to exercise excellent skill in Listen and Support[14].

Skill E - Constancy of Purpose

Dr. Deming said that one of the biggest inhibitors in an organization is the lack of constancy of purpose. Note that purpose is not something that is achieved in the near term. Purpose is the common binding reason the people band together. Both tactical and strategic activities flow from this purpose.

Many organizations do not know what their purpose is beyond staying in business and making a profit. But even this purpose provides minimal stability and guidance if the leader emphasizes it.

Purpose is something team members can believe in and commit themselves to. Purpose allows an organization to be adaptable and flexible beyond just doing the usual. Purpose also allows latitude for the team to be creative and innovative.

Skill F - Define organization principles, sell and administer

Built to Last shows that an organization that knows who it is in terms of values and principles, and sticks to these like a religion, is durable, flexible and rock solid. Imagine an organization that knows its purpose and also knows the values and principles that guide it toward achieving these purposes. This provides the team a structure in which to perform that can be trusted and relied upon.

There is more to be done with the organizational values and principles; they must be preached and sold to the team on a sustained basis. Americans have become cynically aware that leaders come and go every few years so stay tuned and see what the latest preaching is. Principles must be sustained, carried across generations and across many leaders with vastly different personality styles.

---

[14] Refer to Team Member Skills

Skill G,H,I - Constant Improvement

Covey tells about the woodsman who was observed cutting down a tree and had been doing so all morning. When it was suggested that he might sharpen his saw and get the job done quicker and easier, the woodsman said he had not the time for he was busy cutting down the tree. We do this to ourselves all the time - to busy doing to stop and improve our skills, our processes and our ways of doing business.

Constant improvement is something that must be built into the normal flow of activities. If it is not we will be too busy to do it. Nor can it be put off for we are unlikely to ever get back to it. Last it requires patience and a willingness to try, once again, to do better.

Dr. Deming credits this principle with the stick-to-itiveness that allowed the Japanese to work and work and work, until the results are perfection. Obviously real perfection is not expected or really achievable. But it should be obvious if one leader has us regularly improve and another leader does not, then over time the first leader's team will pull far ahead of the latter.

G) Leadership Dynamics and Current Problems

Real problems that the leader encounters are the vehicles for constant improvement. Further the leader is responsible for the development of leaders lower in the hierarchy. Again, the real business situation is the training ground.

H) Leadership Self-examination and Constant Improvement

The leader needs to take a timeout and observe himself at least twice a year. It is recommended to use the Leadership Measurement Tool provided in this book. Using this tool, the leader can pinpoint which skills need further work. Also, the leader should review these self-assessments by leaders lower in the hierarchy.

l) Outside Leadership Assessment and Constant Improvement

Feedback from peers, superiors and subordinates ensure the leader is not delusional. This feedback is need more often than Skill H (above).

Case Studies

<u>Ambitious Albert</u>

The Situation

Albert is a newly hired project manager who is very bright and has a Ph.D, is eager, impatient and ambitious, and doesn't care what he has to do to make his first million dollars. Al is perceptive about the relationship of people in the organization and who has what power.

Ambitious has been given responsibility for a major programming project that is targeted to save the company upwards of a billion dollars a year. Obviously this project has enormous visibility and Al wants the results to be excellent.

In dealing with the project team Al is realistic though demanding. The team has responded by giving him everything he has asked for and more. Ambitious is pleased with the progress.

At the weekly status meetings, Al reports the positive progress in glowing terms. "His team" and "his results" are frequently mentioned. It is clear from what he reports that the project success is directly attributable to Albert.

Albert's manager is delighted and the word is spreading that Al is a comer.

Observations

Ambitious Albert is an excellent performer - right?

Well, yes and no. Obviously the project result Al is getting is just what the organization expects, needs and wants. This is the best of all possible worlds. But it is not Camelot.

Al is showing symptoms of taking all the credit to himself. Al may be a politician that knows how to make things sound good all the while covering the reality of the situation.

It is all well and good that Al is getting positive results if this is the full truth and all the truth. Al should get kudos. But it is the project team, including Al, that deserve the kudos.

An organization that allows, nay even encourages, the notion of the all-powerful heroic manager is not going to develop these people into world-class leaders. Al has that potential but he must be lead beyond his political style.

Next Door Jonathan

Jonathan is a first line manager who has been in his position for three years. Jon has a reputation for meeting his commitments and fulfilling the organization's demands.

His peers and employees like Jon. Many say he is sort of the "boy next door".

Jon is not outstanding and does not speak up usually in management meetings. He gets the work done, his people seem happy enough and life goes on.

There is turnover in Jon's department but not more than the norm for this business.

When managers talk about high-flyers, Jon is not among them. Jon does not stand out either positively or negatively.

Observations

Next Door Jonathan is an ordinary manager getting the work done. This is a very stable situation and not likely to change. Jon is happy. His employees are happy. His manager is happy. Everybody is happy. Life is wonderful.

The only problem is that Jon is not competitive with more capable managers. Jonathan needs to improve. For this to happen, his manager is going to have to intervene and provide the initial motivation for Jon to do something else.

This is a delicate interaction for there is a strong desire to not rock Jon's boat. But this is an example of a situation where if it aien't broke, break it. Jon needs to be lead and nudged.

Rocky Rudolph

The Situation

Rocky Rudolph is a general manager in a small decentralized company. Rocky's organization runs a fish-farming operation that distributes its products throughout the United States and Canada.

In spite of economic pressures, Mr. Rudolph's organization has maintained its business measurements in the green - the same cannot be said for the rest of the company.

Rocky has been giving increasing attention to growing his managers into leaders. He is not sure that this has contributed to his groups business performance but it certainly has not hurt. Rocky is pleased with his group but concerned with where the company is headed.

Recently Rocky visited the company headquarters in St. Louis and was disappointed to learn that the company was developing a plan for a major set of layoffs. These layoffs would not directly affect Mr. Rudolph's group but they did raise some doubt about Rocky's opportunities for promotion in the company. Rocky returned home wondering about the future.

Observations

Rocky Rudolph is the kind of strong, independent leader that most organizations would be delighted to have working for them.

However Rocky's company has a problem with Rocky - his thoughts are beginning to drift towards investigating other alternatives. Rocky needs to have the counsel and advice of his superiors in the company so that he can see why he might want to stay with the company.

It would be a great loss for the company to have Rocky move on but that always is a possibility with a capable independent leader. Rocky needs greater challenges and responsibilities. Providing these is the job of Rocky's leader. Where is he?

Measurement & Interpretation

Leadership can be measured and the measurements provide diagnostic value, i.e. point to appropriate practical improvements.

The greatest leverage for organization development begins at the top with the senior executives and their staffs. Organizations that sincerely want to reengineer themselves have executives who are willing to change behavior.

If we are so fortunate to be able to measure leadership, how do we interpret the results? Leadership has a wide range of performance and appropriate interventions must span and account for these wide differences.

Questionnaire

Our technique here parallels what was done with the teams. First a questionnaire[15] is administered to the people that are managed by the leader. Additionally peer managers may be invited to also provide input but not with the same detail.

There are two sets of questions - both sets are used with subordinates and only one set with peers. These questions do not have a "right" or "wrong" answer. These questions seek to know the best assessment of how the leader is operating now so that the leader can benefit and learn about the effects they are having.

- Questions taking an overview of the impact of the leader.
  - ✓ How effective is this leader?
  - ✓ How satisfied are you with the leader's results?
  - ✓ How well is this leader integrated with a relevant whole?

- Questions taking the view of frequent interactions as a subordinate.[16]
  - ✓ How well does the leader walk like they talk?
  - ✓ How well does the leader reduce fear?
  - ✓ How well does the leader accept only win-win contracts?
  - ✓ How well does the leader increase feedback?
  - ✓ How well does the leader provide a constancy of purpose?
  - ✓ How well does the leader define the organization principles?
  - ✓ How well does the leader constantly improve their skills?

---

[15] See appendix C for the actual questionnaire.

[16] Note that the detail that these questions pursue may also be appropriate with peers of the leader if there is sufficient interaction for the peer to comment.

From the perspective of subordinates or team leadership, initially the most important skills of the leader are those that build trust: walk like you talk, reduction of fear and acceptance only of win-win contracts. These skills allow the subordinate team to continue on their own growth and development.

Scoring

The leadership questionnaire contains ten questions with values[17] of one to ten. A blank response is treated as a zero value.

- Each question is separately averaged across all responses.

- The first three question responses are averaged. This is the **Integration** score (a value between 0 and 10). If the value is between 0 and 5, the Build Trust score is recorded as **Low**; otherwise it is recorded as **High**.

- This completes the scoring for responses of peers and others that have no detailed interaction with the leader.

- The second three question responses are averaged. This is the **Build Trust** score (a value between 0 and 10). If the value is between 0 and 5, the Build Trust score is recorded as **Low**; otherwise it is recorded as **High**.

- The third three question responses are averaged. This is the **Use Strength** score (a value between 0 and 10). If the value is between 0 and 5, the Use Strength score is recorded as **Low**; otherwise it is recorded as **High**.

- Last, the responses to the tenth question, "How well does the leader constantly improve his skills?" is averaged. This

---

[17] See appendix D for Scoring Worksheet and Leadership Summary Report forms

is the **Improvement** score (a value between 0 and 10). If the value is between 0 and 5, the Improvement is recorded as **Weak**; otherwise it is recorded as **Strong**.

The integration score of peers and others not reporting to the leader is used as a sanity check; i.e. to verify that the report of the leader's subordinates is congruent with that of the greater organization. So long as these two reports are within two points of each other, the subordinate's report is used. When the assessment of the subordinates and peers is more than two points then the lesser of the two values is used.

Types

There are eight types of leaders based on their build trust, use strength and integration scores measures as low or high. Each of these combinations produces a particular type of leader that will be further described.

Build Trust	Use Strength	Integ.	*Type of Leader*
L	L	L	Minimal
L	L	H	Politician
L	H	L	Loose Cannon
H	L	L	Country Club
L	H	H	Ordinary
H	L	H	Incependent
H	H	L	Interdependent
H	H	H	World Class

Types Defined

Let's take a moment to understand each of these leadership types.

67

- Minimal

  This type is low in all aspect of leadership. This leader may appear invisible to both her subordinates as well as peers. This person makes no waves and meanders through the business making no significant impact—apparently. Unfortunately even the minimal leader provides leadership by example and in this case the example is one of "do nothing". If allowed to continue, this form of leadership hurts the greater organization by giving credence to this behavior.

- Politician

  The Politician makes a contribution to the greater organization and emphasizes her efforts and content without using their subordinates constructively. The subordinates are viewed simply as "resources" to provide support for the leader and any accomplishments are taken to be those of the leader, not her organization.

  It can be said about the Politician that they understand the larger organization and know how to either contribute or at least appear to contribute. If they have a Minimal superior, even simply the appearance of performance is enough to garner praise, bonuses and promotion.

  Unfortunately the Politician is actively harmful to organizations by down playing the value of their subordinate's contributions and often giving praise, bonuses and promotions to up and coming Politicians alone. This type of leader is commonly found in large organizations since inefficiencies they promote can be hidden behind large numbers - people or dollars.

- Loose Cannon

  This type of manager knows how to use the resources she has been given even while she is not adept at developing these same resources further. This type is not skilled at being perceived as making a significant contribution to the larger organization even if they do. There is a very real potential for this kind of leader to decide to break away from the larger organization and go start her own or join one where she might be in a more powerful position.

- Country Club

  The Country Club type of leader is fun to work for since business pressures are kept low and everyone gets along quite nicely. Unfortunately since this leader does not appear to make a significant contribution to the greater organization her job is at risk. When that happens the replacement leader is likely to be a Politician and offensive to the subordinates. The Country Club hurts the business by lulling her organization into an unrealistic expectation of peace and tranquility.

- Ordinary

  The Ordinary Leader uses well the resources they were given to start with and makes a visible meaningful contribution to the greater organization. This type of leader does not spend much time, effort or attention in developing her subordinate organization. Since most organizations are staffed with competent healthy adults, these staffs tend to sufficiently care for themselves so that the Ordinary leader can continue to function satisfactorily. This is a relatively stable situation. Unfortunately such an Ordinary leader cannot deal with extraordinary situations and the greater organization is at risk when the unusual or unexpected is encountered. But Ordinary leaders do just fine in ordinary times.

- Independent

  The Independent leader knows how to develop her organization and let it run independently while this leader makes their own independent contribution to the greater organization. In many groups this type of manager will be viewed as the "high flyer", i.e. the best of the best. It is an unfortunate organization that settles for this level of performance for it cannot compete with World-Class leadership. But an organization with predominantly Independent leaders will do well and set the average for the Dow Jones stock performance. In the book *Built To Last* organizations with mostly this type of leader are highly admired and respected even while they do not have the superior performance of organizations that are built to last.

* Interdependent

The Interdependent type of leader knows how to develop her organization and then organize this work creatively and constructively. Since they do spend much of their time, energy and attention on these aspects, they may not fare so well in selling the results of their organization. The Interdependent leader is able to run their business on a sustained competitive basis but their achilles heel is how they are perceived in the greater organization. So long as that greater organization is decentralized, then the Interdependent leader will fare well and may even be among the candidates for greater responsibility.

* World Class

The World-Class leader is good for their subordinates, the greater organization and themselves. This leader is able to thrive under all conditions regardless of the challenges presented by the greater organization, tumult of business or confusions inherent in a people-based enterprise. It is from this type of leader that is found the visionary leadership and top performing stocks that are most desired.

Prescriptions

Leadership development requires upper management intervention for all would-be leaders. Practical managers usually ask for a roadmap to tell them what actions should be taken. Given the diversity of the real people providing leadership such a roadmap must be general purpose. Here is such a roadmap:

1. Ask the leader to assess themselves and report where they are.

2. Recognize that superior management decision and action is required to deal with issues of integration.

3. Recognize that some leaders do not fit into the needs of the greater organization and should be removed from that organization.

4. Train the leader consistent with their reported type.

5. Give time for the leader to incorporate the new learnings into their performance.

6. Do this roadmap again.

There are predictable appropriate superior management choices and interventions based on leadership type. The choices and prescriptions center mostly on training though other alternatives are offered.

Leadership Type	Prescription/Choices
Minimal	1. Remove leader from leadership 2. Provide leader valued assignment 3. Train leader in Build Trust skills 4. Train leader in Use Strength skills
Politician	1. Train leader in Build Trust skills 2. Train leader in Use Strength skills 3. Remove leader from leadership is Improvement is Weak
Loose Cannon	1. Remove leader from leadership 2. Provide leader valued assignment 3. Train leader in Build Trust skills
Country Club	1. Remove leader from leadership 2. Provide leader valued assignment 3. Train leader in Use Strength skills
Ordinary	1. Train leader in Build Trust skills 2. Provide leader with Mentor to assist in integrating needed skills appropriately 3. Provide leader with feedback from peers and superiors
Independent	1. Provide leader with valued assignment 2. Provide leader with feedback from superiors and peers 3. Provide mentoring from immediate superior
World Class	1. Train leader in weakest skill 2. Provide leader feedback from peers and superiors 3. Provide leader access to situations where superiors expose their business needs 4. Expand leader responsibilities

Summary

By now we have defined how teams and their leadership operate, how to measure their current level of performance, identify the various types measured, and prescribe action to improve.

Now we turn attention to understanding who is responsible for ensuring the team and leadership skills are acquired and used. By responsibility is meant those who:

- Directly control acquiring and using the skills and therefore do not need anyone else to do something?

- Directly benefit from these skills?

- Would be held accountable for not doing these things by an objective outside third party?

- Have enough specific information to take effective action?

Who Is Responsible?

There are only three roles in a organization that can be responsible - the team, the team leadership, and middle and upper leadership. These roles may go by different titles and multiple roles may be exercised by a single title. Regardless, there are only three roles to consider:

- The Team

  As we already discussed, by a team we mean virtually any group that works with each other on some sort of continuing basis. The only critical aspect of a team is that it be well understood that it is a team and who the team members are.

- Team Leaders

  Team leaders are any persons who are responsible for or who have reporting to them some the team. Some of the titles for this role include team leader, first line manager, department manager or department head. There are many more.

- Upper and Middle Leadership

  Last there is a group of leaders that go by the name of middle manager, general manager or executive. What distinguishes this group is that they have reporting to them team leaders or other middle managers, general managers or executives. In American business this group would also include the board of directors.

Responsibilities

The responsibilities each group depend on:

- The team they are a part of.

  There are many simple teams in any organization. But also note that business managers are often not only leaders of teams but also members of a management team. Thus many managers have both responsibilities as team members as well as team leaders.

- The teams they lead.

  Team leaders may guide one team at a time or multiple teams at the same time.

- The team leaders they lead.

Leading other leaders has its own unique responsibilities.

There is a hierarchy of these responsibilities in which:

- The team is the lowest level of the hierarchy

- The team leader is the next level of the hierarchy and has responsibilities of team leader and management team member.

- The middle management and executive management, including the board of directors in the United States, have all the preceding responsibilities plus unique ones spanning their organization.

Now none of these groups can be expected to assume full responsibility of all these skills until they have had adequate training and opportunity to apply this learning. For analytical purposes, the point where they become fully responsible occurs when they become self-managing, namely when they measure out with an overall score of 5 or greater. Until that point these folks must be coached, counseled and taught by those higher up in the hierarchy.

For the highest levels of executive management where there is no one above them in the hierarchy, they are minimally responsible for recognizing their needs and obtaining these from outside third parties.

Team Responsibilities

The team and each member of the team is responsible for each of the team skills:

1. Listen and Support
2. Value the Whole
3. Fight Fair
4. First Things First

5. Share the Burdens
6. Find & Keep Resources Used
7. Constant Improvement

This responsibility includes:

- Performing these skills

  In other words the exercise and expression of these skills is up to the each team member. They cannot look to anyone else except themselves. All credit or blame for doing these things belongs with the individual team member.

- Training in these skills

  The team is responsible for obtaining training in the skills that the team needs.

- Coaching and counseling other team members

  The team members are responsible for not only using their team skills but also for helping other team member to also do so.

- Assessments and surveys

  The team is responsible for determining when to survey the team skills and who outside the team to include in these surveys.

Last the team is responsible for giving the team leader feedback on her performance. This feedback needs to be based on the actual behavior of the team leader.

This means that the team must be able to discriminate between the behavior the team leader has chosen and the actions required of the team leader by the greater organization.

The team leader can only be held responsible for what she has control over - namely the behavior she has chosen.

There may be other opportunities for the team to comment on actions by the greater organization but these should not be dumped on the team leader as the only available scapegoat.

Team Leader Responsibilities

In addition to the team skills, the team leader is responsible for the leadership skills.

A) Walk Like You Talk
B) Reduce Fear
C) Accept Only Win-Win Contracts
D) Increase Feedback
E) Constancy of Purpose
F) Define Organization Principles, Sell and Administer
G) Constant Improvement

This responsibility includes:

- Performing these leadership skills

    The team and the greater organization depend on the team leader to perform these skills. All credit or blame for exercising these skills is that of the team leader.

- Training in these skills

    The team leader is responsible for obtaining training in the skills that she needs.

- Assessments and surveys

    The team leader is responsible for determining when to survey the team and his peers or outside groups.

In addition the team leader is responsible for giving her team feedback on their performance. This feedback needs to be based on the actual behavior of the team and not that of the team leader, the organization or other groups.

Executive Leader Responsibilities

In addition to the team skills and the team leader skills, the middle and executive leader is responsible for two skills that cannot be otherwise exercised.

- Developing Organizational Support for Teams and Team Leaders

  Organizational support for teams and team leaders may include the gamut of organization functions but might especially include:

    ✓ An appraisal system recognizing the unity of the team and their consequent joint performance.

    ✓ Salary, bonus and promotion systems recognizing the business value of teams, team development and associated sophistication with these skills.

    ✓ Provide funding for the time to perform surveys and to use the results.

- Obtaining support from outside the organization to support the needs of the teams and team leaders. Some examples include:

    ✓ Identification of consultants that can provide training, coaching and counseling on the team and team leader skills.

✓ Purchasing or having developed tools that minimize team and team leader overheads including those involved with performing surveys.

Getting Started

"OK", you say, "you have me convinced about these skills but I cannot change my organization by myself. Where do I start."

Here are the places where everyone can get started, set an example and engage the participation of others. These actions need only occur within the normal scope of your existing job responsibilities.

- Survey

  How are you doing with your own skills? How is your team doing? If you are a leader, how are your teams doing?

  By getting data out in the open, it becomes possible to show and to convince ourselves and others to take action. Without data, it is much harder.

- Educate

  Part of the reason that so little action takes place on these skills is simple ignorance. Educate yourself and then share this with your peers. With such education comes an appreciation that there is a real opportunity to do better and that what needs to take place is within our own capabilities and control.

- Train

Train yourself on team member skills starting with "Listen and Support". Use this skill and train others. This skill is revolutionary in its effects and influence.

- Sell

  Carry the messages about team skills and leadership to all that you work with as part of your ongoing desire to help yourself and your business to be more productive and competitive. Be the first on your block.

Well that's all but it's a mouth full. As Nike might say, "Just do it". Any action on your part is better than leaving this material to rattle around in your head or worse on a book shelf. Action backed up by measurable data and the predictable interpretations presented here provide the basis for small successes. These then add up over time to produce significant contributions and remarkable changes that none of us would ever predict.

- Improve

  Project management technology uses a term "Lessons Learned" that applies here. As you attempt to use what you have learned about team and team leader skills take some time either by yourself or with colleagues who you are working with to assess:

  ✓ What has worked well?

  ✓ What has not worked so well?

  ✓ What conclusions are supported from the data obtained from the first two questions?

✓ What recommendation do you have for yourself in proceeding?

If you take the time to learn as you go and document these learnings, then you will get better. We must then adapt, adjust and accommodate to what we have learned. By taking brief time outs to determine what successes and near successes we have achieved we will give ourselves realistic feedback, guidance and supporting data to go forward.

Appendix A - Team Performance Questionnaire

This questionnaire is your personal, private assessment of the performance of a specific team with specific team members.

If you are part of this team, please answer all ten questions.

If you are the manager or team leader of the team or if you are outside the team, please answer only the first three questions.

A response of 1 means a **Low Level** of performance and a response of 10 means the **Highest Reasonable Level** of performance and not the highest ever conceivable. If the team has no performance on an item or you are unsure of the performance, please skip the item and your response will be treated as a zero value.

Please write directly on the questionnaire and clearly circle your responses.

<u>Team Performance Questionnaire</u>

Team Name:

_____

Date: _____

Question #1	**How productive is this team?**
Answer	**1 2 3 4 5 6 7 8 9 10**

Question #2	**How satisfied are you with the team results?**
Answer	**1 2 3 4 5 6 7 8 9 10**

Question #3	**How well integrated is this team with the greater organization?**
Answer	**1 2 3 4 5 6 7 8 9 10**

Question #4	**How well does the team listen and support?**
Answer	**1 2 3 4 5 6 7 8 9 10**

Question #5	**How well does the team value the whole?**
Answer	**1 2 3 4 5 6 7 8 9 10**

Question #6	How well does the team fight fair?
Answer	1 2 3 4 5 6 7 8 9 10

Question #7	How well does the team put first things first?
Answer	1 2 3 4 5 6 7 8 9 10

Question #8	How well does the team share the burdens?
Answer	1 2 3 4 5 6 7 8 9 10

Question #9	How well does the team find and keep resources it uses?
Answer	1 2 3 4 5 6 7 8 9 10

Question #10	How well does the team constantly improve?
Answer	1 2 3 4 5 6 7 8 9 10

Appendix B - Team Performance Scoring and Reporting Forms

Scoring of the Team Performance Questionnaire entails calculating the average reported values for the team members on each question separately, i.e. sum all answers to question 1 and divide by the number of reported values and then do this for each question.

For questionnaires reported by non-team members, only the first three questions are reported and calculated.

The following summary sheet is provided to assist in performing these calculations.

Team Performance Questionnaire
Scoring Form

Average for Question # 1	
Average for Question # 2	
Average for Question # 3	
Average for Question # 4	
Average for Question # 5	
Average for Question # 6	
Average for Question # 7	
Average for Question # 8	
Average for Question # 9	
Average for Question # 10	

Average for the averages of questions 1, 2, 3 (Enter in Report as Integration Raw Score)	
Average for the averages of questions 4, 5, 6 (Enter in Report as Inclusion Raw Score)	
Average for the averages of questions 7, 8, 9 (Enter in Report as Synergy Raw Score)	
Multiply the three averages of averages together.	
Divide the result of the multiplication by one hundred. (Enter in Report as Overall Report)	
If the average for question 10 is less that 5, enter a **Weak** otherwise enter a **Strong.** (Enter in Report as Ability to Improve)	

<u>Team Reporting Form</u>

Date of Survey: _____

Details

Integration Raw Score	
Inclusion Raw Score	
Synergy Raw Score	

<u>Notes From Feedback Session</u>

_____

_____

_____

_____

© Ken Boggs, 2002
371 River Road
Pittsboro, NC 27312
Phone: (919) 932-7933
Email: jkennethboggs@mindspring.com

Team Name: _____

Summary

Overall Report	
Team Type	
Movement Toward Improvement	

Follow-up Actions Planned

_____

_____

_____

_____

_____

_____

_____

Appendix C - Leadership Performance Questionnaire

This questionnaire is your personal, private assessment of the performance of a specific leader or manager.

If you are subordinate of this leader, please answer all ten questions.

If you are the superior or a peer of this leader, please answer only the first three questions.

A response of 1 means a **Low Level** of performance and a response of 10 means the **Highest Reasonable Level** of performance and not the highest ever conceivable. If the leader has no performance on an item or you are unsure of the performance, please skip the item and your response will be treated as a zero value.

Please write directly on the questionnaire and clearly circle your responses.

<u>Leadership Performance Questionnaire</u>

Leader Name:

Question #1	**How effective is this leader?**
Answer	**1 2 3 4 5 6 7 8 9 10**

Question #2	**How satisfied are you with the leader's results?**
Answer	**1 2 3 4 5 6 7 8 9 10**

Question #3	**How well integrated is this leader with the greater organization?**
Answer	**1 2 3 4 5 6 7 8 9 10**

Question #4	**How well does this leader walk like they talk?**
Answer	**1 2 3 4 5 6 7 8 9 10**

Question #5	**How well does this leader reduce fear?**
Answer	**1 2 3 4 5 6 7 8 9 10**

Question #6	**How well does this leader accept only win-win contracts?**
Answer	**1 2 3 4 5 6 7 8 9 10**

Question #7	**How well does this leader increase feedback?**
Answer	**1 2 3 4 5 6 7 8 9 10**

Question #8	**How well does this leader provide a constancy of purpose?**
Answer	**1 2 3 4 5 6 7 8 9 10**

Question #9	**How well does this leader define organization principles, sell and administer?**
Answer	**1 2 3 4 5 6 7 8 9 10**

Question #10	**How well does this leader constantly improve?**
Answer	**1 2 3 4 5 6 7 8 9 10**

Appendix D - Leadership Performance Scoring and Reporting Forms

Scoring of the Leadership Performance Questionnaire entails calculating the average reported values on each question separately, i.e. sum all answers to question 1 and divide by the number of reported values and then do this for each question.

For questionnaires reported by peers and superior leader, only the first three questions are reported and calculated.

The following summary sheet is provided to assist in performing these calculations.

Leadership Performance Questionnaire
Scoring Form

Average for Question # 1	
Average for Question # 2	
Average for Question # 3	
Average for Question # 4	
Average for Question # 5	
Average for Question # 6	
Average for Question # 7	
Average for Question # 8	
Average for Question # 9	
Average for Question # 10	

J. Kenneth Boggs

Average for the averages of questions 1, 2, 3 (Enter in Report as Integration Raw Score)	
Average for the averages of questions 4, 5, 6 (Enter in Report as Build Trust Raw Score)	
Average for the averages of questions 7, 8, 9 (Enter in Report as Use Strength Raw Score)	
Multiply the three averages of averages together.	
Divide the result of the multiplication by one hundred. (Enter in Report as Overall Report)	
If the average for question 10 is less that 5, enter a **Weak** otherwise enter a **Strong.** (Enter in Report as Ability to Improve)	

Leadership Reporting Form

Date of Survey: _____

Details

Integration Raw Score	
Build Trust Raw Score	
Use Strength Raw Score	

Notes From Feedback Session

_____

_____

_____

_____

_____

Team Name: _____

Summary

Overall Report	
Team Type	
Movement Toward Improvement	

Follow-up Actions Planned

_____

_____

_____

_____

_____

_____

_____

Bibliography and Book Review

Age of Discontinuity, Peter F. Drucker Harper and Row, Inc., 1968

This is a blast from the past. It is amazing that Drucker could see so clearly what has developed. This book, though a bit of heavy reading, is worth the time to slow read and ponder. There is much Drucker has described that is even now emerging.

Built To Last - Successful Habits of Visionary Companies, James C. Collins and Jerry I. Porras, Harper Business, 1994

This is an excellent exposition and analysis of what it takes to make a corporation super successful and able to endure for long periods of time. The emphasis is partly on "values" and is consistent with ordinary intuition, i.e. that those who warrant the label of "visionary" are doing something special consistently. This is a must read, understand and apply for all corporate executives as it clearly lays out what stands leadership must take.

Celestine Prophecy, James Redfield, Warner Books, Inc., 1993

This is a short, entertaining novelette that makes recommendations about how to "grow up" and how to interact with a more sophisticated and "grown up" society. It is a hokey book in many ways but what it has to say, mostly seems right on the money. In particular, the "Eighth Insight" describes a level of communication that can be observed in high performing teams.

Deming Management At Work, Mary Walton, G.P. Putnam's Sons, 1990

This book presents nonstop case histories illustrating the value and benefit of Dr. Deming's 14 points. This is an excellent source of practical, real-world examples of how to succeed.

Deming Management Method, Mary Walton, G.P. Putnam's Sons, 1986

This book defines and elaborates Dr. Deming's 14 points. This is an excellent source for these very important guidelines.

The Digital Economy, Don Tapscott, McGraw Hill, 1996

This is an excellent overview of the ongoing revolution in Western-influenced business, worldwide. The changes that are occurring make obsolete all that has gone before and these changes are happening at "light speed". There is no way to avoid the consequences of these changes and thus this is a must read for those whose ambition is to survive in business in the 21st century.

Empowered Manager: Positive Political Skills At Work, Peter Block, Jossey-Bass Publishers, San Francisco and Oxford, 1990

This book is the first one specifically directed at middle management, i.e. managers of managers and which are not parts of the executive levels. Taking up this much-maligned group and giving them hope and leadership is difficult. This book offers many ideas and solutions. In so doing, it tends to be a bit pedantic and boring. Nonetheless, it is a valuable resource.

Empowered Teams - Creating Self-Directed Work Groups That Improve Quality, Productivity and Participation, Wellins, Byham and Wilson, Jossey-Bass Inc., 1991

This book could be used for a semester course in how to decide to implement self-managing teams. It could also serve as the basis for senior management training before implementation. It is a bit too pedantic for worker-level general usage. Nonetheless this is an excellent, well thought through volume with much useful material.

Empowerment - Definition and Measurement, TR 29.1349, J. Kenneth Boggs, IBM Corporation, 1992

This paper describes what is meant by empowerment and illustrates these definitions with anecdotes and analysis. This paper brings together much of the established ideas on the subject of empowerment but then extends them by comparison and contrasting against existing management techniques and styles.

Empowerment - Notes and Current Learnings, TR 29-1506, J. Kenneth Boggs, IBM Corporation, 1992

This paper develops further the concepts and practices of empowerment defined in TR 29.1349 (see above).

Oregon DOT Paves Way With Self-Directed Teams, Article in March 1995 edition of Public Sector Quality Report, pages 3-5.

This is the first report that includes dollarized tangible savings through use of self-managing teams.

- Reduction of supervisory costs by more than $1.2 million annually.

- Improvement in customer evaluation of quality of DOT roads.

- Slashing of overtime by 58%.

- Trimming equipment repair costs by $60,000 annually.

All is not rosy. There are challenges in developing an appraisal and payment system. Too there are challenges in interfacing these self-managing teams into a hierarchical organization.

Shortcomings aside, the DOT's results are impressive enough that they won a 1994 "Innovations in State and Local Government" award (including a $20,000 prize from the Ford Foundation.

Applying Object Technology Lessons Learned On The OOTC Mentoring Practice, Overhead transparencies, George Yuan, IBM Object Oriented Technology Center, August 1995

George Yuan has much practical experience in both successful and unsuccessful object oriented programming projects. In his anecdotal material a requirement is defined for a management approach different from what is commonly available. On an exception basis, some IBM management have tentatively and for limited terms been willing to experiment with Mr. Yuan's proposals. Others working in this area support Mr. Yuan's experiences and reports.

Principles of Scientific Management, Fredrick Winslow Taylor, Harper and Brothers Publishers, New York and London, 1911

This book is the seminal writing and thinking surrounding the most prevalent form of organization in the United States currently. It is strange that our thinking is stuck by this work that is approaching being a century old. Have we learned nothing since?

Regardless this is an essential reading for it gives clear explanations and draws stark lines of action and responsibility. It is dated and somewhat arrogant but up front.

Self-directed Work Teams - A Primer, Torres and Spiegel, Pfeiffer and Company, 1990

This is a short, concise introduction to empowerment and self-directed organizations. It is excellent and could be used as a textbook for developing self-managing teams, i.e. as a point to start a constructive discussion.

Self-directed Work Teams - The New American Challenge, Osbourn, Moran, Musselwhite, Zenger and Perrin, Business One Irwin, 1990

This book is an excellent "bible" for a facilitator. It provides numerous examples and gobs of useful information but it is not easy to get through and would overload most people.

Self-managing Teams, TR 29-2082, J. Kenneth Boggs, IBM Corporation, 1995

This paper defines and elaborates what a "self-managing" team means.

Seven Habits of Highly Effective People, Covey, Simon and Schuster, 1989

This book provides and excellent proposal for a principle-centered individual much like that proposed by Collins and Porras for corporations. This book contains numerous anecdotes and examples. It is easy to read but challenging to do what it recommends.

Succeeding As A Self-Directed Work Team, Harper and Harper, MW Corporation, 1992

This is an excellent workbook that could be used as a training text in the development of a self-managing team. It contains a very useful list of companies and their successes with these approaches.

Workplace 2000: The Revolution Reshaping American Business, Joseph H. Boyett and Henry P. Conn, Penguin Books, NY, 1991

This book is excellent thinking but slow reading. It explores all the major topics of the "new workplace". IBM gave a copy to everyone in its organization even though IBM does not have this new workplace.

This book could be used as a college course textbook but it is weak on the subject of empowerment.

Zapp! The Lightning of Empowerment, William C. Byham, Ph.D. with Jeff Cox, Harmony Books, NY, 1988

This book is most entertaining and a very quick read - two hours tops. It is in story form and rapidly explores the viewpoint of both the employee and the first line manager. Many clear, specific and useful observations and recommendations are made. The book is short on complete exposition and rationale but is inspiring if somewhat simplistic.

Index

About the Author

Ken Boggs retired from IBM Corporation after nearly thirty-eight years in a range of management and professional assignments. His career spanned the creation of ubiquitous large system computing, international information systems networks, the Internet, and the accreditation of project management.

Ken is a certified project manager and a qualified Myers-Briggs consultant. He has worked with small teams and some very large ones while managing projects up to $5M in value. Ken currently is a project management mentor and provides selective consulting and Myers-Briggs counseling.

Ken is married to Mary Lucas, physical therapist and yoga teacher, and lives in rural Chatham county North Carolina. When he is not working with teams, Ken is an avid putterer - building on his ten acres of pine and hard woods, gardening, operating an amateur radio station KB4RV, exercising and doing yoga, playing backgammon, singing folk songs and playing guitar, and enjoying his growing entourage of grandchildren.

www.ingramcontent.com/pod-product-compliance
Lightning Source LLC
Chambersburg PA
CBHW051421280526
45785CB00003B/1111